Voice of the Primordial Buddha

A Commentary on Dudjom Lingpa's Sharp Vajra of Awareness Tantra

By Anam Thubten

Voice of the Primordial Buddha

A Commentary on Dudjom Lingpa's
Sharp Vajra of Awareness Tantra

By Anam Thubten

Third Edition 050525

Cover Design and Interior Art Work: Will Cosgrove
Book Design: Laura Duggan

Hardback: 978-1-7320208-8-7
Paperback: 978-1-7320208-6-3
Ebook: 978-1-7320208-7-0

Table of Contents

AUTHOR'S PREFACE

Throughout the process of writing this text, my heart was filled with joy. Some of the joy came from sitting and writing as a creative work; at other times, it felt like the joy was coming from a much deeper place in my consciousness that I couldn't comprehend. It felt like I was reconnecting with a source that is so sublime. Strangely, I felt like I was reconnecting with my roots, whatever that might mean.

I developed a deep affinity with Dudjom Lingpa at an early age. I belonged to a monastery in Eastern Tibet where he had lived for many years. I had the thought now and then, while walking on the grounds of that monastery, that Dudjom Lingpa also walked on this ground, which gave me the sense of sacredness everywhere in that monastery. As time went by, my affinity with his lineage continued to grow in my being. As human beings, sometimes we have an intuitive feeling that we have a strong connection with a tradition or a person, a connection that is not just adventitious but one that comes from an unknowable source. In other words, an auspicious karmic connection. I feel that I have such an auspicious karmic connection with Dudjom Lingpa and his lineage, which goes beyond my ordinary comprehension. Thinking of this brings waves of joy in the sea of my consciousness. Therefore, there was always a strong desire within me to offer some contribution to his wisdom teachings.

When Tulku Jigme Wangdrak Rinpoche, the fourth descendent of Dudjom Lingpa, asked me to write a commentary on the most sacred text from Dudjom Lingpa's revelatory writings, I felt extremely honored with his trust. I felt that my affinity with Dudjom Lingpa was taken to a whole new level.

Let me take this as an opportunity to express my utmost gratitude to His Holiness Khenpo Jigme Phuntsok, Lama Garwang, Lama Tsurlo, and many other wonderful Dharma teachers who blessed my mind.

I'm very thankful to Tulku Jigme Wangdrak Rinpoche for being a catalyst for me to write this book. I'm also very grateful to Laura Duggan, who put her heart and so much effort into editing it.

May all beings be awakened to their true nature as the unborn Buddha.

Anam Thubten

Note on Language Conventions

Tibetan words are presented in phonetics followed by Wylie transliteration in parentheses. While Anam Thubten's pronunciation is a Tibetan dialect from Golok, in this text the phonetics are the more commonly known Lhasa pronunciation. For Sanskrit terms, diacriticals are omitted, adding an "h" after "s" or "c" when the pronunciation requires it. In general, only the first occurrence of any foreign word is italicized.

Short Biography of Dudjom Lingpa

Dudjom Lingpa (1835–1903) is one of the most celebrated Dzogchen masters in the Nyingma tradition of Tibetan Buddhism. He was an extraordinary terton, or treasure revealer, who revealed many teachings and sadhanas from the realm of enlightened mind and visions that go beyond the ordinary intellect. Many people became enlightened in one lifetime from studying with him as well as by practicing in his lineage.

He was born to a nomadic family in a region called Serta in Eastern Tibet. At some point, he left his hometown and journeyed to another region in Eastern Tibet known as Markog, where he began to teach. He became well known there. Later he returned to his home region and created a *gar*, which is a community of yogis and monastics living together. Later, that very site became the place where His Holiness Khenpo Jigme Phuntsok built the Larung Gar monastery, the largest monastery in Tibetan history.

It is said that Dudjom Lingpa did not have any human gurus. He received all the wisdom teachings from visions in which buddhas, deities, and masters appeared, such as Avalokiteshvara, Manjushri, Padmasambhava, Yeshe Tsogyal, and Longchenpa. He was considered self-awakened, which makes him unique among other well-known Tibetan masters. When he was alive, not only did he discover many revelatory teachings, he also taught extensively, reaching the hearts and minds of many.

He had a family and children who became well-known male and female masters carrying his lineage forward. His descendants and lineage holders have a reputation for being both good Dharma masters as well as really good people, such as the Third Dodrupchen, Tulku Drimed Ozer, and others. Today, his living descendants continue to carry his lineage.

As a yogi, he never wanted to have a permanent monastery or residence; therefore he changed his residence quite often. Later, some of his residences became monasteries. He encouraged many of his students to be wandering yogis, and sometimes he told them to go to specific destinations to meditate, some of which were quite far away, thus spreading his lineage throughout Tibet. Today even in the Western world, there are Dharma teachers and sanghas that continue to spread and preserve his lineage.

Voice of the Primordial Buddha

A Commentary on Dudjom Lingpa's Sharp Vajra of Awareness Tantra

INTRODUCTION

Tibet is a unique country geographically. It is situated at the highest altitude in the world, which earned it the name "the roof of the world." The landscape is breathtaking, with diverse topography, from thick forests in Eastern and Southern Tibet to vast canyons and deserts in Western Tibet. It is filled with beautiful lakes and snowy mountains. Not only is nature enchanting there, but Tibet's history is extremely colorful and rich. It often captures the attention of others with awe and mystery. Tibet developed its own Buddhist culture with its own unique traditions, such as the tradition of revelatory writings known as *terma* (W. *gter ma*), which is not very well known in other Buddhist traditions.

The great masters who discovered revelatory writings are known as *tertön* (W. *gter ston*), or treasure revealers. Some of their names are still uttered with great reverence, and their teachings are timeless, embraced by people today long after the terton has been gone from the world. Dudjom Lingpa (1835–1903) was undoubtedly one of the most important tertons in the twentieth century; he was both original and visionary, which is apparent in his teachings. His life was also very unique. He was one of the few people whose awakening did not come from traditional Buddhist training. As he stated, "I've never had a human guru." Usually, people study the traditional classical treatises and then practice Vajrayana and the Dzogchen tradition with a living master.

Almost every Buddhist master has taken that approach. Yet even though Dudjom Lingpa didn't have any gurus, he had visions in which buddhas and masters gave him teachings. At some point, he started writing down these termas, and it took some time for the public to accept their authenticity. In the end, he became a most renowned terton, and countless students came to him to receive teachings—lay people, monastics, yogis, high lamas, and so forth. He is regarded as one of the greatest Dzogchen masters of the Nyingma tradition.

Dudjom Lingpa was not only a great terton, but he taught extensively, giving oral commentaries on his revelatory writings. There would be a huge archive of his oral teachings if someone had had a recording device at that time. One of his disciples, Yukhok Chatralwa, studied with him for a period of time. He wrote down Dudjom Lingpa's oral teachings as personal notes. They were quite accurate and almost sounded transcribed since they contained some slang words that Dudjom Lingpa used. Of course, there are no recordings, but those notes are a window into the personality of Dudjom Lingpa as well as his teachings. There are other tertons who offered many revelatory writings but did not teach as extensively as he did.

Dudjom Lingpa was one of the great Dharma lions, and if the student was ready, he was able to give them the "heart of the matter" right away. It is said that some of his students studied with him for only a short period of time, then became wandering yogis spending the rest of their lives practicing what they learned without feeling they missed anything. The insight they received from him became the basis for life-long spiritual practice, which led to profound awakening.

Today, his lineage is very alive, and there are sizable communities practicing in his lineage in Tibet and beyond, including sanghas and individuals in the West. Some of his revelatory writings have been translated into various languages including English. This book, a contemporary commentary in English on Dudjom Lingpa's writing, can help people understand his unique teachings, as well as Vajrayana and Dzogchen in general.

These days, I feel there are not enough contemporary commentaries on Vajrayana and Dzogchen in English and much work needs to be done in this area. Commentaries in English would not only raise awareness of the sacred teachings in the Western world, they would also benefit people everywhere, including Asia, as English is becoming a universal language. There are many cases where young people from places like Bhutan cannot understand the Buddhist writings in their language but can understand them in English. This is just the beginning of a trend. If we cannot bring the teachings to life in English, many of them will eventually be lost forever or merely preserved in a digital library somewhere, with no one left who can read them. This may sound exaggerated but time will tell.

Dudjom Lingpa's text is not considered just scholarly writing but rather a tantra, which are words of a buddha, such as Samantabhadra. Often tantras are filled with cryptic language, and sometimes they are extremely dense and pithy. This *Sharp Vajra of Awareness Tantra* by Dudjom Lingpa is presented in such a style. Often a commentary is required for readers to understand a tantra. It would be quite difficult to understand it right away simply by reading the text on its own. Therefore some of his students wrote Tibetan commentaries on his text. Their translation can be useful to illuminate the tantra. Yet for modern readers, an even more contemporary commentary is needed. I hope that this book can fulfill such a task.

The Sharp Vajra of Awareness Tantra encapsulates the entire Buddhist path, all the way to Ati Yoga, or Dzogchen, the nondual tradition of Tibetan Buddhism. The main theme of this text is Dzogchen, and it describes the path of Dzogchen in a nutshell with very potent language. It brings together all the Dharmas, or paths, beautifully into Dzogchen as the ultimate yoga, the highest Dharma. Dzogchen is considered the most direct shortcut to enlightenment. It points out the absolute truth within each of us and its techniques are direct and not complicated at all.

Many people have had profound insights from reading Dudjom Lingpa's text. The text deals with both the doctrine and the practice of Vajrayana, especially Dzogchen. In that sense, it is a complete explanation of these paths. It is not just a philosophical text that has no practical instructions. Nor is it some kind of practice manual that is lacking an explanation of the underlying philosophy. This is a perfect book for those who want to understand the doctrine of the Vajrayana and Dzogchen and engage with the practices.

There is a growing interest in Dzogchen everywhere, including the West. In the past, Dzogchen was kept secret for many reasons. Yet the times as well as people are changing, and it feels that today Dzogchen should be widely taught and made available to the world. Of course, this should be done with great care.

His Holiness Khenpo Jigme Phuntsok was the greatest Dzogchen master in our time. I hold him in my mind as Buddha and Padmasambhava. He was someone who was not only awakened but had extraordinary wisdom that could see things that ordinary intelligence does not foresee. I witnessed that personally. When His Holiness came to the West, in some of his lectures he encouraged people to practice Dzogchen. To me, that was his way of giving permission to make Dzogchen available to a larger audience. He must have seen that many people are ready to understand it, and that it would be of great benefit.

If you are inspired to study or practice this text, each time you begin, you might like to sit in silence and pray with total sincerity, not allowing the mind to be distracted by any thoughts during the prayer. In your mind, invoke the Primordial Buddha and set the aspiration to realize the nature of mind, or the profound wisdom of Vajrayana or Dzogchen. Then every word from the text will create a crack in your consciousness. Sometimes you may see that opening happen immediately and other times, you may recognize it only after it has happened.

When you begin reading this text, you may come across some places where you feel you totally understand it and other places where you don't understand it at all. This is a very natural process. If you come back and keep reading it again and again, soon a new level of understanding will dawn upon you. That understanding will not be merely intellectual but rather a very profound insight that will turn your frame of reality inside out.

Each verse of Dudjom Lingpa's text is like a golden box carrying so much meaning. Therefore, as a reader, sometimes you might like to read just one verse and its commentary, then sit with it, letting it sink into your mind. This book is more than a book of information that you read just once and be done with. Instead, it is a book that you can continually come back to throughout your life. When you are not reading it, you can cherish it as a sacred object on your altar, knowing that this tantra by Dudjom Lingpa is there for you.

The Title

From the wisdom web of sacred vision,
The original purity, the expanse of Samantabhadri,
Spontaneous presence, the treasury of the
Great Completion,
The Sharp Vajra of Awareness Tantra,
The quintessence of the Great Secret Mantra.

The Tibetan tradition places a great deal of importance on titles. They are regarded as the window through which the whole body of a teaching can be summarized. There is even the notion that if someone is quite ready, with the right state of mind and heart, she or he only needs to read the title to get the entire knowledge of the text. It seems safe to say that among all the Buddhist cultures, Tibetans developed a very elaborate system for titles. Some of them are quite long and fancy. As part of the tradition, Tibetans make sure that the title is in harmony with the content so that readers can have a very clear idea about what is in the text.

This text, which is generally called the *Sharp Vajra of Awareness Tantra*, has an entire verse as its title, which turns out to be unique. There are only a few other Dzogchen texts that have a lengthy verse as a title. This can be regarded as an expression of the creativity of Dudjom Lingpa's revelatory writings, which are very original in their language and often praised for their creativity by many masters.

Often toward the end of a title for a text, including this one, there is the expression *zhuk* (W. *bzhugs*), which means resides. *Zhuk* is also an honorific term that might be applied to residing like kings and queens, or spiritual figures like venerable Dharma masters. When it is used in the title of a text, it creates a mental impression that turns an inanimate object into something animate, so that people feel that such a text is not just an object but is alive and full of blessings. They feel devotion and reverence to the text, knowing that by reading it, they will receive a blessing that will transform their consciousness. In that sense, Dharma texts are not considered spiritless objects or just letters written on paper. This is also why people in the Tibetan Buddhist culture would not throw the sacred texts on the floor and would not step or sit on them. The texts are placed in a high place, like an altar, wrapped in beautiful silk with a fancy wooden cover on both sides.

Tibetans also feel the text is like a vessel through which they can hear the voice of past spiritual luminaries, such as the Buddha or spiritual masters. If you live in today's world, obviously there is no way you can see Shakyamuni Buddha teaching a profound sermon at Vulture Peak Mountain. That extraordinary event is long gone—over two thousand years have passed since that time. Yet devout Buddhists sometimes feel a poignancy and longing to witness such an event, a nostalgia, wishing that they could be there. That longing can be quenched by simply coming across one of the *Prajnaparamita Sutras,* which are the recorded teachings on emptiness that Buddha delivered on Vulture Peak Mountain.

In fact, all Buddhist monasteries have a similar sacred object on their altar: a copy of the Buddhist canon. There is so much respect for the texts that they believe that even sacred statues of Buddha should never be placed on the texts. There is a logic behind this. Observing the sacred images of Buddha, you may not have any communication with the Buddha. But if you read the sutras, you may feel you are communicating with him and listening to him in person.

Many tantras are attributed to the Buddha or the Primordial Buddha, Samantabhadra. Again, readers can feel that they are directly hearing the voice of Samantabhadra, even though Samantabhadra is just an expression of one's pure luminous consciousness.

The first line of the title tells us that this is not just an ordinary text but a revelatory teaching, or terma. A terma is a treasure revelation that always originates from a dimension of mind that goes beyond the intellect. The Nyingma tradition, the oldest tradition of Tibetan Buddhism, respects termas, or revelatory writings, many of which are attributed to Padmasambhava as the source of the inspiration. Padmasambhava has a very special place in the hearts of Tibetan Buddhists because he brought Tantric Buddhism from ancient India to Tibet.

There are also different categories of terma that describe the different vessels through which the writings come to the terton, the treasure revealer. Sometimes people literally have visions in which they see sacred forms or syllables that inspire them to write a terma. Sometimes finding a mysterious object from the natural world triggers an eruption of spontaneous writings. Other times, an entire teaching just pours out spontaneously as if the terton is in some kind of "zone" where creativity just flows on its own. Those teachings are written down while the terton is totally in union with enlightened mind and the writing flows without any effort.

An important phrase in the first line of this title verse is "wisdom web of sacred vision," which refers to a genre of terma that this text belongs to. Dudjom Lingpa's followers categorized his revelatory writings into two, three, and sometimes four genres. The methodology for creating these genres has to do with the source, or catalyst, for such writing to manifest in his consciousness. For example, the source of many of his writings lies in a variety of visions he had, such as visions of Manjushri, in which he felt he had direct communication with the deities. Those visionary encounters with the deities became a powerful conduit for his revelatory writings. The title is stating that this text belongs to that genre of revelatory visions.

If you were around Dudjom Lingpa while he was giving teachings, you would be utterly amazed by his spontaneity. He wouldn't have to think or look at other texts for reference. His words would not be repetitive or have mistakes. He would teach as if he were reading from a beautifully composed text, but he would not be reading anything. His words were an outpouring of profound teachings from a source beyond the matrix of mundane mind.

In this opening, Dudjom Lingpa is stating that the realm from which he received this text is the "expanse of Samantabhadri." Let's spend some time exploring this. In Tantric Buddhism, the Primordial Buddha is called *Adibuddha*. In the tantras of the Nyingma school, Samantabhadri is the Primordial Buddha in a female form; there is also a male form of the Primordial Buddha, Samantabhadra. The Primordial Buddha is not to be taken as an individual Buddha, such as Shakyamuni Buddha, nor held as a deity. The true Adibuddha is regarded as the nature of mind that is primordially, intrinsically pure and sublime. Dudjom Lingpa is saying that this text is neither scholarly nor coming from his intellect but comes from a state of consciousness that is enlightened.

The "expanse of Samantabhadri" is a very beautiful expression. It is the realm of what is called the luminous nature of mind. This is also known as the *dharmakaya*, the highest level of buddhahood, which lies within each of us. In general, Vajrayana, or Tantric Buddhism, encourages us not to seek the buddha outside. Vajrayana texts warn us that we will never find the true buddha by searching for it outside of ourselves. Instead they invite us to look inside. They teach that the true buddha lies within each of us, pointing out that the luminous nature of our mind is the true buddha, the dharmakaya, regardless of what name we give it. We can call it Samantabhadri.

People often have an unconscious belief that even though the true buddha or luminous nature of mind does not lie outside, it must be some kind of sublime, exalted state of consciousness that is inaccessible in the present moment, since the present moment feels so ordinary to them. Or some people may think that the luminous nature of mind, dharmakaya, or other notions are too transcendental, like quasi-religious phenomena that have no real application in their life. But all these ideas come from not truly understanding these concepts.

Tantric Buddhism, especially Dzogchen, skillfully invites us to experience the luminous nature of mind, or dharmakaya mind, in the realm of *now*. This can leave us with a feeling of amazement, seeing that it is so simple and is always present in us. Here, Dudjom Lingpa is saying that this text comes from the luminous nature of mind. One could say that when he was ready to write, he was in the "dharmakaya zone," and he just revealed the entire terma without any effort.

The Yanas—Spiritual Vehicles

Try to imagine that you are traveling somewhere for a specific reason—you are on a tour, or a business trip, or going to a family reunion. In the beginning, you have the plan to travel, which you put in your schedule, and you know where you are going...that's always important. Then, in the modern world, you have numerous options for getting to your destination. If it is far away, you may need to fly. If it is close, you could take a car, or sometimes even a bicycle, or go by foot. Even going to the same destination, the speed of your travel is dependent on your capacity and the means that you are using.

Imagine you are going on a holy pilgrimage and decide to visit Mt. Kailash. Of course, the truth is that if your mind is enlightened, wherever you are is always a holy site. But imagine that you begin the pilgrimage far away from Mt. Kailash. You could take an airplane, drive a car, or hike. It is the same destination but the speed and experience will be completely different depending on how you travel.

In the same way, even though all Buddhist paths are aiming for the same destination—nirvana, buddhahood—the methodologies of each path and tradition differ from each other. And one's experience of the journey would be unique.

In Buddhism, the path, the practices, and the experience of the journey are part and parcel of what are called *yanas,* or spiritual vehicles. It is said that there are numerous yanas because of the complex nature of our mind. Yet they are systematized and put into categories, which gives rise to a general understanding or overview of the yanas. The most well-known categories of yanas are the two yanas, Hinayana and Mahayana. Each of these systems is practiced by individuals with their aspiration to be free from samsara, either for oneself or for everyone in the world. The word *samsara* is one of the most common terms in all of Buddhist writings. Its etymology refers to a life or world with perpetual suffering, like a wheel that continuously turns.

Hinayana is called the small vehicle, a spiritual path based on the motivation of seeking enlightenment only for oneself, not for all living beings. Mahayana is motivated by the desire to seek enlightenment for the benefit for everyone.

Within Mahayana, there are two further yanas, known as Prajnaparamitayana (the Transcendent Wisdom Vehicle) and Vajrayana (the Diamond Vehicle).

There are major distinctions between the yanas. For example, Hinayana is built upon the premise that life with all its pleasures is something to be cautious about, because it could be a trap that binds you to samsara—endless misery. Therefore, many of the practices are often based on controlling and restraining one's senses and behavior. Hinayana does not emphasize developing a strong relationship between oneself and the outside world.

This is not true in the Mahayana tradition. Perhaps the bodhisattva best epitomizes the path of Mahayana, which is to engage with the world and everyone in it; to develop a heartfelt connection with everyone; to help the world to the best of one's ability; and to learn as much as possible from life, including the sorrows of the world.

The Hinayana approach is not utterly obsolete because it works for many who are just starting out on the path to enlightenment. For some, their state of mind is not ready to embrace the path of Mahayana. It's like somebody who is learning how to swim. She might not be ready to be a lifeguard immediately. She is learning how to float on the water, do different strokes, and so forth, and she may find it very joyous just to learn such an amazing skill like swimming. Once she starts to really enjoy swimming, she may move from the pool to the ocean. Then she may realize she doesn't want to swim just for herself. She may then want to become a swimming instructor or even a lifeguard. Now her skill is not just for herself; now she is ready to offer her skill for others. This is the essence of the Mahayana path.

The very premise of Vajrayana is that enlightenment can be discovered now, in this very life, in your own flesh and bones. Its main view is that the world is sacred. This is not just a random statement. Vajrayana as a tradition has built an edifice of literature and treatises containing a litany of reasoning to support this very view. Many of the practices in Vajrayana are designed to alter our consciousness to develop such perception. For example, in many liturgies, known as *sadhanas* in Vajrayana, you visualize that you become the deity, the world is the mandala of the deity, the four directions are sacred mandalas filled with deities, and your perception of the world is transformed. You maintain the remembrance that every form you see is a *kaya*, or sacred form; every sound you hear is a sacred sound, or *mantra*; and every experience is *jnana*, or sacred wisdom.

The Vajrayana doctrine influenced many of the cultures in the Himalayas, and you will find instances of this view in everyday mundane life there as well. Some of them may not be Vajrayana doctrine but are folk beliefs and stories that have direct roots in Vajrayana. For example, if you grow up in Eastern Tibet, you may believe that when a cat purrs, she is not just making an animal sound, but that she is actually reciting the Tara mantra. This is one of many examples.

In the title, Dudjom Lingpa is pointing out that this teaching belongs to Dzogchen, or the Great Completion, which is considered the highest yana in the Nyingma tradition. This title is also stating that this text is on Vajrayana, or secret mantra, especially the path of Anuttarayoga Tantra, the Unsurpassable Yoga, the highest path in Vajrayana.

Great Secret Mantra

Vajrayana is often called the secret mantra. Often the tantric masters interpret *secret* with two meanings: concealed, or in Tibetan, *gab* (W. *gab*); and hidden, in Tibetan *bé* (W. *sbas*). *Concealed* is stating that the meaning of Vajrayana is difficult to understand. Only individuals with a certain mindset or capacity can understand the wisdom or truth of Vajrayana, which is so profound. *Hidden* means that Vajrayana can sometimes be misunderstood, and that some people may misuse its techniques. Conventional society may even develop a negative attitude toward its techniques because they appear quite unconventional or provocative. In ancient times, the tantric adepts, known as *mahasiddhas,* taught Vajrayana in a special environment only to a handful of disciples who they thought had the capacity to understand such a path.

The tradition often encourages students to have the readiness to enter such a path. Because of that, Vajrayana postulates the importance of working with a guru, known as a Vajra master, who has a set of noble qualities—someone who has gained deep understanding of the tradition and who is purified and evolved so that she or he would not cause harm to the disciples nor lead them astray.

The relationship to the Vajra master is like a relationship between patient and doctor. This is a useful analogy because the Dharma, or spirituality is often depicted as nectar, or *amrita*. The real meaning of amrita is the medicine that heals one's ills. Imagine someone has a serious physical illness. They could go to a local pharmacy to get over-the-counter medicine without needing a doctor's prescription. But such medicine may not heal the root illness, and then the patient will need something more powerful, which requires consulting with a doctor and going through a thorough analysis so the doctor can prescribe the right medicine. This analogy can be applied to the way Vajrayana works for people.

The second part of the term *secret mantra* is mantra. Mantra here is more than the usual mantra that is recited, such as the name of a deity. Mantra refers to the entire Vajrayana path, but not only because Vajrayana uses mantra as part of its path. Mantra has a wider meaning that encapsulates the power of Vajrayana. Buddhist scholars give the etymology of mantra by splitting it into two: *man* means mind, *tra* means to liberate. So here, *mantra* means "that which liberates the mind." Basically, the term *secret mantra* is postulating that Vajrayana is a path with the power to liberate us.

The Panoramic Scope of Tantra

As we said, the title is the window through which you can look at the entire body of this text. This text is regarded as a tantra. *Tantra* is a Sanskrit word, which can be interpreted as a continuum, or web. Tantra is not one single thing but a whole variety of themes, all of which fall under the umbrella of tantra.

The best way to understand the panoramic scope of tantra is by dividing it into three categories: causal tantra, method tantra, and resultant tantra. The *causal tantra* refers to the luminous nature of mind, which is the unconditioned state of our mind or consciousness that is primordially enlightened. For those who are not enlightened, this luminous nature is obscured by the veils known as adventitious stains, a simile for internal conditioning. This unconditioned state of mind is the primary principle of Vajrayana. *Tantra* means continuous: the unconditioned, luminous nature of mind is always continuous and always remains in us, as if an endless divine river, a ceaseless stream, is flowing in the realm of our consciousness, regardless of what we are going through.

Method tantra refers to all the techniques and practices that developed under the tantric umbrella, which are means to arrive at the full awakening to that luminous nature of mind, or methods that lead one to perfect buddhahood, or the state of Vajradhara, the Primordial Buddha. Unlike many other systems, tantra is like a treasury of numerous transformative methods and practices, such as mandala creations, mudras, offerings, yogic conduct, and other radical techniques. They are all connected under the umbrella of tantra as part of one powerful and transformative web.

Resultant tantra means that all adventitious conditioning is completely purified and the highest fruition, or the goal of all tantric practices, is actualized, so that the forever-residing luminous nature of mind is fully uncovered or manifested. It is no longer veiled. It is like the sun shining brilliantly in the sky without any clouds obscuring it. This analogy is saying that the sun was there all along, temporarily veiled by clouds. Similarly, the luminous nature of mind always resides in our consciousness regardless of the conditions we are going through or what state of mind we are in—happy, unhappy, wholesome, unwholesome, liberated, not liberated, and so forth. The luminous nature of mind has no beginning and no end. It belongs to the unconditioned.

Buddhism often divides everything into conditioned and unconditioned. Unconditioned is anything that goes beyond our mental, intellectual comprehension. Anything that is unconditioned cannot have a beginning or an end. In this context, resultant tantra is complete awakening to luminous nature of mind, which has no end. It can be called ceaseless, even though it is not a thing that we are referring to. *Ceaseless* is an imaginative way to describe the transcendent quality of the luminous nature of mind, or the state of Vajradhara.

Vajra Mind

The essential title of this text is *The Sharp Vajra of Awareness Tantra*. This title uses the phrase, *shé rig dorjé nön po* (W. *shes rig rdo rje rnon po*), which appears to be a very unique expression not often used. It has a brilliant meaning that captures the very quintessence of the Vajrayana as well as Dzogchen teachings.

The Tibetan word used here for *awareness* is *shé rig* (W. *shes rig*). In general Buddhist treatises, shé rig is synonymous with mind. It can also be translated as consciousness. But shé rig has to be interpreted in context. The etymology of shé rig is that which is cognizant and aware. By itself it does not refer to nature of mind nor enlightened mind but simply mind.

Regarding its use in this title and its association with *dorje nonpo*, or sharp vajra, *shé rig* refers to the mind or consciousness that is freed from all conditions and returned to its true nature that is originally pure and unconditioned. That awakened mind is also wisdom that directly sees the true nature of all things, where the duality of knower and known is transcended.

So even though the term *shé rig* often refers to mind or consciousness, the best way to translate this word *shé rig* in English in this context, is with the word *awareness* so that people don't conjure up the unenlightened mind, the samsaric consciousness.

Vajra (Tibetan: *dorjé*) has many meanings such as pure, sacred, indestructible, unborn, and unconditioned. In this context, it also refers to the enlightened mind that is the indestructible union of awareness and emptiness. That enlightened mind is also like a divine weapon. In the ancient liturgies, a vajra is sometimes mentioned as a divine weapon that is indestructible and can destroy all the forces of opponents or anything that exists. The title is saying that awareness, or the awakened mind itself, is a wisdom which, like a divine weapon, destroys the forces of duality, delusion, and suffering.

The Homage

To the supreme Lord of all enlightened families and mandalas,
Buddha nature, I pay homage with undying devotion.

Both Indian and Tibetan Buddhist texts almost always have a verse of homage in the beginning. It is such a well-established standard that it would be unusual not to have words of homage in Tibetan writings. These words become the window through which the reader can see the genre and the subject of the text. Sometimes the homage is also the way the writer shows his or her utmost devotion to the source of wisdom, or lineage masters that have relevance to the theme that she or he is writing about.

Yet it is not always true that the object of such homage is a deity or master. For example, in the well-known text called *Madhyamakavatara*, or *The Way of Madhyamaka*, the author Chandrakirti writes a hymn to compassion as the opening stage for the text. In it, he praises the power of compassion as indispensable for one's journey to enlightenment.

During the translation of the sutras at Samye Monastery, under the reign of the Tibetan King Trisong Detsen, the translators and *panditas*, or scholars, came together and created standardized guidelines for the homage in the beginning of texts attributed to Buddha. They decided, for example, to add a line of homage to Manjushri if the text belonged to the Abhidharma, homage to Shakyamuni Buddha for texts that were part of the Vinaya, and homage to the buddhas and bodhisattvas if the text belonged to the sutra *pitaka*, or basket.

In general, authors tend to write verses in the beginning of their texts that are homage to their *ishtadevata*, or personal deity, Buddha, or their own guru, whomever they have strong devotion or faith toward. These verses of homage are a way for an author to express his or her devotion to the sacred and also point out that the writing is rooted in a reliable and noble source.

In this text, the verse of homage reveals the very nature of the text, which belongs to Vajrayana. This verse is paying homage to buddha nature in the form of a tantric deity, the lord of the mandala. These two terms—*buddha nature* and *lord of the mandala*—will be explained below.

Buddha nature is a critical concept in the general Mahayana tradition, although the way different traditions interpret it varies. Some schools of thought define buddha nature as our innate potential to become enlightened. However, in Dzogchen, buddha nature is more than our potential to become enlightened. Instead, it is the primordial nature of our mind that is pure all along, not stained with the adventitious conditions of the *kleshas*. Because its nature has never been conditioned by anything, it is already enlightened. It is often described as luminous and is expressed as the dharmakaya by Dzogchen masters. We will explain dharmakaya a bit later in this book.

One analogy for buddha nature is the royal mirror covered with dust. Even though this precious royal mirror hasn't been used, is covered with dust, and doesn't reflect any images, there is not one single moment when it is not a royal mirror. The dust does not alter its nature. Yet the covering of the dust blocks the surface of the mirror so it doesn't function as a mirror outwardly. The moment the dust is wiped away, the royal mirror can once again reflect images. The royal mirror represents the nature of our consciousness, which is intrinsically pure in itself. Even though our consciousness is veiled by incidental conditioning—mainly the three kleshas, or poisons, of greed, hatred, and ignorance—its primordial nature is always pure. Many terms have been developed to express this primordial state of our own mind, such as natural purity, or buddha nature.

The notion of buddha nature fundamentally conveys the message that there is inherent goodness in each of us. But it is not an original goodness that is now lost. Buddha nature is more than the original state of who we are—it is the ground of who we are in this very moment. In that sense, we were never separated from it in the past, we are not separated from it now, and we will not be separated from it in the future. It always remains as the very basis of who we are.

Dzogchen masters emphasize that this is not a theory but a living truth that anybody can experience. In fact, the goal of Dzogchen, Mahamudra, and all other nondual traditions in Buddhism is to experience this as soon as possible and not be sidetracked by anything else. These traditions also teach that since buddha nature is always there, we don't have to search for it anywhere else. With the right state of mind, we can discover it right now, on this very spot.

In this verse of homage, buddha nature is depicted not only as an ishtadevata, or deity, but the lord of enlightened families and mandalas. The term *mandala* often refers to a variety of things, but the literal meaning is a circle, a configuration, or assembly. A mandala can be regarded as a congregation or gathering of ishtadevatas. The best way to understand a mandala is to create a visual representation of it. Let's try to imagine in our mind a regal assembly where the king or queen, the sovereign lord, sits on a golden throne, surrounded by ministers, retinues, bodyguards, and so forth, in a grand palace, which is situated in the center of a vast kingdom, composed of many regions and tribes.

Let's use that visual image to depict the form of the sacred mandala. In that sense, the sacred mandala is a gathering or assembly of ishtadevatas, or deities. The lord of the mandala is like the king or queen who presides over the entire palace and beyond—the whole kingdom. The other deities, who come from enlightened families like Padma, Karma, etc., are like the chieftains, ministers, noble people, and subjects, who surround the presiding lord.

In the end, the mandala is just a visual representation of our enlightened mind. The five Buddha families—Vajra, Ratna, Padma, Karma, and Buddha—are a representation of different aspects of the same enlightened mind. In the tantras, the lord of the mandala is often given a name such as Buddha Vajradhara, or Buddha Samantabhadra, even though they are not supernatural deities. It is important not to externalize or anthropomorphize them. We should never underestimate our tendency to turn these representations of the pure nature of mind into a thing or real deity. When that happens, another attachment is added to bind our consciousness further in the trap of duality.

Here, this verse is portraying buddha nature in the form of the Primordial Buddha who is ruling this sacred kingdom, the mandala. This verse is expressing the utmost devotion to buddha nature in the form of the lord of the mandala, as well as establishing the very basis of this text, which deals with the themes of Vajrayana, especially Anuttarayoga Tantra, the Unsurpassable Yoga.

I. Taking the Impure Mind as a Path

Within the equality of the three: samsara, nirvana,
and the path,
Empty, all-pervasive, pure space,
I, the great dharmakaya yogi, freed from the extremes,
Will illuminate how the magical display of wisdom
appears as potential energy:

The opening stage for this text is choreographed in the form of a play or event where the Primordial Buddha is about to deliver a discourse. It first describes the place or the perfect environment where the Primordial Buddha is ready to teach under providential circumstances to the right audience. This verse describes the place, who is teaching, and the time of the teaching.

An opening stage is ubiquitous in the scriptures of both sutras and tantras. Many people are familiar with this type of opening in Buddhist sutras such as the *Heart Sutra*, one of the most recited Buddhist sutras. In the *Heart Sutra*, it said that Buddha was ready to deliver a profound discourse, and the place was Vulture Peak Mountain, which is considered a sacred site. It is not an imaginary location but a physical place situated in Northern India, where many pilgrims go even today. Nor was Buddha a metaphorical being but a physical being. In his audience were monks, nuns, and Shariputra, one of the main characters, who was a historical person and student of Buddha.

The Place

Here, in the initial setting in this text, neither the place nor the master are in fact physical. The place is not an actual place nor is the master an actual person. The place or environment where this discourse takes place is the nonphysical space. It is the realm of the ultimate truth that is free from all duality or any possible limitations, not bound to time or place, where nirvana, suffering, and the path from samsara to nirvana do not exist separately. In some sense, this is very close to the notion of the great emptiness in the Mahayana tradition, or the *dharmadhatu*, the source of all. Dharmadhatu and the great emptiness are often referred to as space, or *kha* (W. *mkha*) in Tibetan, a metaphor that captures their characteristic as that which is limitless, without boundary, and all pervasive. Here, pure space can be regarded as the realm or place where the Primordial Buddha is speaking.

In other writings, a place is often used as a metaphor for dharmadhatu or emptiness. For example, in the *Life of Padmasambhava*, Padmasambhava encountered the Indian King Indrabodhi, who was very impressed by his presence. Out of curiosity, the king asked the young man, "Who are you, where are you from, what do you do, and who are your parents." Padmasambhava replied, "My father is the wisdom of primordial awareness. My mother is Samantabhadri, bliss-emptiness. I am from *chö ying kyewa mé pa* (W. *chos dbyings skye ba med pa*), the unborn dharmadhatu. I belong to the caste of the nonduality of space and awareness." Here you can see that Padmasambhava is not answering the question in an ordinary way. Otherwise, he would say, "So and so is my mother and father; I belong to a certain caste like brahmin or untouchable." He is answering from the point of view of ultimate truth, and yet his answer is accurate, perhaps the most accurate description of himself. He is saying that he is from the place called dharmadhatu. This is the very place where the Primordial Buddha is about to deliver this discourse.

The place where the Adibuddha, or the Primordial Buddha, delivers the discourse is also called *Akanishtha*, which is a non-physical realm. One could say that it is standard for Tantric Buddhist scriptures to start with an extraordinary opening in which the Adibuddha gives a profound discourse to an audience in a certain place, but none of this is physical. In the Vajrayana

Tantras, the teacher, the Primordial Buddha, or Adibuddha, is also known as the Dharmakaya Buddha.

The Three Kayas

The dharmakaya is one of the three kayas, which, along with sambhogakaya, and nirmanakaya, are the main principles in Vajrayana. Not all Mahayana traditions use the same language to describe them. Some language is much more nondual than others. For example, in Dzogchen, the three kayas are described as purely states of one's own mind.

The three kayas are a way of describing the state of enlightenment, and there are very rich doctrinal systems that describe them. In the general Mahayana systems, dharmakaya is often described as the purified state of our consciousness that transcends all characteristics, beyond any conditions. It refers to the very essence of enlightened mind. All Mahayana schools agree that dharmakaya is beyond words and verbal descriptions. It can never be fully expressed in words and can only be realized by enlightened mind itself.

While dharmakaya has no form, sambhogakaya is usually described as a buddha with form and characteristics. It is depicted as a buddha (or buddhas) who presides over the mandala and who forever turns the wheel of the Dharma to the assembly of sublime beings. Sambhogakaya is beyond birth and death, and some forms of sambhogakaya appear as sacred visions to bodhisattvas.

Nirmanakaya is often the physical manifestation of a buddha or buddhas, such as Shakyamuni Buddha, a physical being born in this world, a real person who became enlightened and turned the wheel of Dharma, teaching the way to liberation.

This description of the three kayas is the general Mahayana doctrine. The Dzogchen description of the three kayas is quite different. The three kayas are no longer envisioned outside oneself but are different states of mind. This points out once again that the very nature of our consciousness or mind is already perfect and enlightened in itself. Dharmakaya refers to the essence of our mind that is empty. Sambhogakaya is the luminous nature of the mind. Nirmanakaya is the unhindered capacity of the mind.

Here, the verse is stating that there is no separation between the three kayas. The Primordial Buddha is the embodiment of all of them. The three kayas are described not as physical beings or entities but as the nature of one's mind. Therefore, buddha nature is the embodiment or union of the three kayas, since it is none other than the pure nature of mind that is always perfect from the beginning.

The Teacher, Buddha Samantabhadra

In that sense, the master who is about to turn the wheel of Dharma, or deliver the most profound discourse, is buddha nature, the Dharmakaya Buddha. The master or the Buddha who is speaking here is not a historical Buddha like Shakyamuni. Instead, it is the Adibuddha, the Primordial Buddha, sometimes called Samantabhadra, Samantabhadri, or Vajradhara.

But the question is, who is Buddha Samantabhadra? The tantras say that Buddha Samantabhadra becomes enlightened before anyone else, without needing to purify one speck of karma nor cultivate any virtue. Buddha Samantabhadra is sometimes called the first Buddha, which may give one the idea that he is a real individual, who happened to be somewhere, sometime long ago, like "once upon a time," and became enlightened, became the first Buddha, purely out of good luck. The whole presentation on Adibuddha can give such an idea. But this would be quite inaccurate.

Buddha Samantabhadra is actually a representation of true enlightenment in which our mind is simply being awakened to its original nature that is already pure and luminous. In that sense, Buddha Samantabhadra represents such true enlightenment rather than the enlightenment of one person and goes beyond any framework of time, place, or individual.

The members of the audience for this discourse are not human beings but are manifestations of the Primordial Buddha. This is another major difference between the setting in the *Heart Sutra* and this tantra. In the *Heart Sutra*, the master and students are individuals separate from each other. Yet here, there is no duality between master and students. The enlightened mind is simply speaking to itself.

The Time of Original Purity

Again, as a reminder, the opening verses are describing the place, who is teaching, and the time of this teaching. The time is the perfect time, which is not ordinary time but is the transcendence of time, known in the Nyingma Tantras as *kadak gi dü chenpo* (W. *ka dag gi dus chen po*), the time of great original purity. Often this notion of transcending time is described as that which goes beyond the three times of past, present, and future. This invites us to let go of any thoughts about this opening setting as something historical or happening in real time, with a particular location, and with a particular person. Instead it is all taking place in the realm of nonconceptuality.

This makes sense since this whole discourse is an expression of enlightened mind itself. The time of great original purity is something that even many Buddhist intellectuals had a hard time understanding, so much so that some of them even refuted the concept. In their minds, logically thinking, even though they negate the intrinsic nature of time, if there is time, it should fit into the rigid box of past, future, and present. To transcend all of that and then accept the concept of "the time of original purity" definitely perplexed their intellect. They would say that if there is no time, then what is the time of original purity. They are taking the word *time* literally, not with a transcendent view.

So this time of original purity is not really time. Yet it is called time, which may sound very contradictory. Sometimes such contradictions can help us to transcend all mind-manufactured reality, including time. Time does not really exist. Automatically, people always associate any kind of activity with doer, agent, time, and space. It is a habit of our brain. Our brain has a hard time making sense out of anything without using the conceptual framework of time. If you look around in the mundane world, you can point out the conceptual framework for all events and activities that happened, are happening, or will happen—from the most major event to the smallest event. But transcendent time invites us to rise above this paradigm, to be in touch with transcendence, which in Buddhism is called the unconditioned.

Why is this teaching indirectly inviting us to be in touch with such a transcendent place and time in the very beginning of the text? The purpose is once again to help us engage with this revelatory writing not from the point of view of our usual paradigm, which is called the conditioned, but to engage with it from the unconditioned. Then we will be ready to understand the most profound truth that this text offers us.

The Nature of Reality

Here Buddha Samantabhadra is giving this profound discourse on the nature of reality in which all duality is transcended, inviting the whole world not to go somewhere else but to return to the original state of all things. The original state of all things is the unconditioned dimension of reality. Try to imagine that the nature of reality is like the sky, free from all limitations, naturally spacious, unhindered. Suddenly clouds come and veil the sky completely so that not even a space the size of a palm can be seen. The original state of all things is like the sky before it is hidden by the veils of clouds. In that original state, there is no separation between enlightenment, imprisonment, or the path from imprisonment to freedom, which is expressed in the verse here as the "equality of the three: samsara, nirvana, and the path." Even though the original state of all things is obscured, it has never changed and has never been lost. It is always there whether or not our mind can recognize it. So the possibility of returning to that original state is always present and available.

The ground dharmakaya, buddha nature,
Freed from the extremes, endowed with the
three liberations, is primordially enlightened.

The original state is sometimes known as dharmadhatu, the source of all, a notion held in all Mahayana traditions that is often described with different categories to convey its nuances. For example, it is said that dharmadhatu, the nature of reality, is endowed with three gates of liberation. The three gates are sometimes translated as emptiness; signlessness, or absence of characteristics; and aimlessness, or absence of expectations. In Mahayana and Vajrayana, these three gates of liberation are the transcendent nature of all things, where all conditions, even the law of karma, are transcended.

Bear in mind that these categories cannot be explained in only one way because they are taught in Abhidharma as well as in Mahayana sutras. Each system gives a totally different explanation for them. The category of the three gates is also used in Vajrayana, and this verse is a perfect example of that. Many masters also give original interpretations of the three gates of liberation based on their own understanding, so their definitions cannot be rigidly held as the absolute definition.

The three gates of liberation are perhaps the most important theoretical fulcrum in all of the Mahayana traditions. Ultimately, the three gates are one inseparable gate, and each is a nuance of emptiness, the most essential principle in Mahayana. The three gates are considered the only way that one can reach nirvana, or enlightenment.

Imagine in your mind that enlightenment is a beautiful city with a royal palace, beautiful parks, and temples. Its citizens are endowed with riches beyond imagination. The city is fortified with impenetrable walls in four directions. There is only one grand entranceway that one must go through to get inside. This image could be used as a metaphor for the relationship between the three gates of liberation and enlightenment. Nirvana is like the beautiful city, and the three gates of liberation are the entranceway.

Let's take some time to go over the three gates of liberation. The first is *emptiness*, or sunyata. The term is a negation that indicates void or lack of something. In deep inquiry into the nature of all things, the realization arises that there is not even one single phenomenon that has *svabhava*, or intrinsic nature. *Emptiness* means phenomena are devoid of such intrinsic nature.

To our unexamined perception, everything seems to have intrinsic nature. Let's look at a car. To our mind, there is a car that is a real, singular, autonomous thing that is separate from everything else in the world. Everyone agrees that the object in front of us is a car, without any question. But if you examine it closely, there is no such thing. If you open the hood, you can say, "Where is the thing called car?" but you will not find any carness. There are only parts, and the whole thing is named *car* only by us. If you inquire further, even those parts are just like *car* itself; you cannot find any of them—hood, tire, all the way down to molecules. The whole thing becomes unreal, and there is no solid ground for car. But this is not how our mind perceives it. In such inquiry, we come to the realization that *car* is just a concept, a label, that our mind superimposes through ignorance of the true nature of reality. With that realization, then we experience emptiness as the true nature of everything that we can see, feel, think, touch, and so forth. Emptiness is the truth of all things as being empty of svabhava.

Signlessness is the true nature of all things unconditioned by our mental designations called signs. Signs are the separate characteristics that we assign to everything we perceive in the world. Imagine you are seeing or thinking of an object like the car. Your mind perceives the car as a collection of patterns that are separate from everything. In your mind, that object is a car, not a house or any other object. In your mind, that car might be a sedan, with a red color, with a specific aerodynamic shape, and four seats. But the whole thing is a mental construct onto which you are adding conceptual signs—color, shape, size, numbers, and other specific characteristics. None of them exist in the realm of the nature of reality. That is signlessness, and that is the truth of all things.

Aimlessness means that our idea of attainment is also a mental construct. Usually life is full of aims, whether secular or religious. For example, we have a strong idea that we are here, and there is something we are going to achieve either in the near or far-distant future. It could even be enlightenment. In this way, our mind makes enlightenment something solid, an entity that is separate from right now, something to be attained in the future. And there is a "me" who is a separate person moving toward achieving such a goal. But the whole thing is an illusion. Aimlessness is the truth that completely dissolves this illusion.

In the expance of the union of the three kayas, the display of spontaneous presence,
The display of the inseparability of disciple and master,
Appears to myself and those who are equally fortunate
As the glory of our excellent karma, aspiration, and merit.
For individuals who do not have the fortunate karmic propensity,
There is nothing to gain or obtain on this path, just like paintings of food.
This is the domain of the fortunate individuals.
This sky-treasury of dharmata is their sublime father's legacy.

Even though everyone possesses buddha nature, it is said that without having auspicious and advantageous conditions coming together, one would not find the path nor become awakened. Finding a path and the right spiritual guide requires a variety of factors that are more than just good luck. Even more auspicious circumstances are needed for someone to find advanced teachings or have the chance to enter the higher path. This very text is a precious, priceless, rare treasury revelation transmitted from enlightened mind, which one would not discover nor understand unless one had some extraordinary, auspicious karma, causes, and conditions. This text illuminates Vajrayana, especially Dzogchen, and it is said that Vajrayana itself is so profound that it would be a rare time and place for individuals with such karmic circumstances to even have the opportunity to come across it. There are many analogies and reasonings that postulate this very fact.

For example, in a very well-known liturgy, *Prayer in Seven Chapters to Padmasambhava*, there is a dialogue between King

Trisong Detsen and Padmasambhava in which Padmasambhava spoke of the rarity of Vajrayana. He said that among all the eons in this world, there are only three times when the buddhas taught the Vajrayana path. Padmasambhava said even 840 million buddhas have not taught it. While this is not to be taken literally, Padmasambhava is pointing out that Vajrayana is profound and precious, and one has to have a certain aptitude, readiness, and all the right circumstances to enter such a path.

We could also use beautiful metaphors, such as the *udambara* flower, which is mentioned in ancient liturgies. It blossoms only in rare and extraordinary circumstances and does not last for a long time. We could say that this path is like the udambara flower.

Vajrayana is not only difficult to discover without the preparatory fortunate circumstances, it also can be very tricky in terms of misunderstanding or misusing it. Discovering Vajrayana is compared to attempting to steal the jewel on the head of a poisonous snake, which is quite a powerful image to conjure up.

If you are reading this book, please do not get scared by this analogy. Do not think that maybe you are one of those people who lacks the prerequisites to receive such profound teachings. Instead, this verse might inspire you to entertain this logic: the fact that you are reading this text could be a sign or indication that you have the right karma and readiness to practice this path. Otherwise, you might not even come across this book.

The Sky-Treasury

Dudjom Lingpa is also stating that he did not write down the text from his own intellect; rather, he tapped into his own enlightened state of mind from which this very text arose. He described such an enlightened state of mind as the "sky-treasury of dharmata." The sky-treasury is an expression in Buddhist writings for something that is inexhaustible, such as inexhaustible riches or inexhaustible enjoyment. He is saying that he tapped into a state of mind that is like an inexhaustible source of all the Dharmas.

As an original and prolific terton, he demonstrated that he was always tapping into that state when he wrote or taught. There is a famous anecdote about Dudjom Lingpa and his son, the third Dodrupchen, Jigme Tenpai Nyima. Jigme Tenpai Nyima was a very well-known scholar who wrote volumes of texts. In fact, one of his texts was presented to the thirteenth Dalai Lama, who was said to be impressed by its scholarship. At one point, Jigme Tenpai Nyima and his father, Dudjom Lingpa, had a philosophical dialogue that lasted for a few days. Others who witnessed the dialogue between father and son reported that Dudjom Lingpa was speaking spontaneously and didn't stumble on any point. He made a comment toward the end of the dialogue, saying to his son, "Your intellect is like a bag of barley flour, or *tsampa*, which gets less and less as you eat it. My sky-treasury of Dharma is infinite and can never be exhausted." This humorous conversation between father and son is showing that he was tapped into that state.

In this verse, Dudjom Lingpa is saying that as the transmitter of this text, he is offering it to those who are the right recipients, like offering an inheritance, which evokes a wonderful feeling. It is very personal, intimate, and inspiring, giving the feeling to practitioners or disciples that they are about to receive a precious inheritance, one that they deserve. They are worthy to receive such gifts.

The supreme master, Samantabhadra,
universal sovereign vajra,
Manifests the miraculous display of disciples.
Listen, disciples, nondual potential energy of
awareness itself:

As you read this chapter, you may think the opening scene is like a divine symposium in which the Primordial Buddha Samantabhadra is about to deliver the most profound discourse that anyone ever delivered in the entire universe. A symposium is not even a good example since it is too finite to capture the grandness. Maybe another image to conjure up is a scene from some science fiction movie where there is an intergalactic assembly of representatives from different planets coming together, and in the middle of it, the presiding master or leader gives a speech on unity, peace, harmony, or the discovery of the mystery of the universe. Such an image can evoke the grandness of this setting.

So obviously there should be an audience, just as there is for any other gathering. But again, one must remember that this whole scene is a nondual phenomenon. There is no duality between the master and the audience. Indeed, the whole audience is the pure miraculous manifestation of the Primordial Buddha. Yet because this whole discourse is arranged in the format of a dialogue, this verse indicates that the Primordial Buddha is ready to speak. He is even demanding attention from the audience. "Listen,…" it says.

Such a demand from the master is quite prevalent in both the tantras and sutras. For example, in the sutras Buddha often said these words before beginning a discourse: "Pay attention carefully and memorize it." This phrase, on the surface, is quite easily understood—the teacher is simply beseeching the audience to pay attention. But there is more to it. In this context, the teacher is asking the audience to open their hearts and minds with devotion and surrender, and to be ready to embrace something so profound that it might challenge their concepts. It is more than asking someone to listen to an intellectual discourse but rather to listen from the heart. In that way, transformation can occur in the audience of listeners.

Here, the enlightened mind is just speaking to itself. As readers, we should imagine in our mind that we are there right now. We are sitting in that intergalactic symposium, feeling such overwhelming joy from being fortunate enough to hear the most profound discourse, the secret of enlightenment that we have been waiting to hear for a long time.

Buddha Samantabhadra is asking us directly to pay attention and listen carefully. As a reader, you should not read this as another philosophical text but read it with an open heart, receptivity, and even surrender.

Potential Energy

The last line of the verse points out again that the disciples are not separate from the master, which is the enlightened mind. Disciples are merely the display of *tsal* (W. *rtsal*), or the potential energy of primordial awareness, or *rigpa* (W. *rig pa*).

Potential energy is one of the most important terms in Dzogchen. It describes the unhindered, unobstructed, vibrant quality of the enlightened nature of mind from which and in which anything can manifest. It is full of boundless potential. Fundamentally, Dzogchen teaches that everything that you can see, smell, taste, touch, and conceive—that which has form and that which is totally mental—arises from an origin that is not any "thing" that we can point to with our finger. Everything emerges from primordial awareness, which is a state of our mind that is totally unconditioned.

The primordial mind is sometimes referred to as *bodhicitta*, such as, for example, in Longchenpa's famous writing, *Chö Ying Dzod*, or *Dharmadhatu Kosha*. Dzogchen teaches that the reason why all perceived or conceived things can arise from bodhicitta, which is none other than the pure state of our consciousness, is because our original awareness, rigpa, is not dead but fully alive. That aliveness is the potential energy, or tsal. It is alive and unhindered, which means anything can arise from it. In other words, it is the energy, or strength, or dynamic prowess of that bodhicitta, which itself is undefinable. It is the ability to manifest, perceive, experience, and create.

This whole notion is a unique narrative about how our existence comes into being, and not just existence but perceived existence. We can describe this narrative as a very positive outlook on everything we perceive because it traces everything back not to delusion or some primordial flaw but to bodhicitta, which is always positive and sacred.

The narrative keeps getting better. Longchenpa, following the Dzogchen Tantras, again and again says that everything appearing in our five senses is an ornament to *ying* (W. *dbyings*), the dharmadhatu. The term *ornament* may not have a serious religious meaning, like virtue or sin, but it undoubtedly has an inspiring meaning. It is often associated with something that is beautiful or that beautifies, something that is not to be rejected but to wear, show, or display. In essence, Dzogchen invites us to have a truly transcendent outlook in which we see that everything we experience in this life arises from bodhicitta, and we embrace everything as ornaments of dharmadhatu, the primordial space.

Analyze the chief of the three gates [body, speech, and mind]—the all-creating king.
Recognize the form and color of the all-creating king.
Analyze its origin, residence, and destination to find that it has no place and is transparent.
This is spontaneously present in the true nature of the path of cutting through.

Now the actual discourse begins, which is not just a theoretical discourse but rather a series of contemplations that enables one to realize the actual nature of mind. One question that may arise now is, "What is the use of understanding the nature of mind?" This is obviously a reasonable question.

The answer is that all of samsara, the vicious circle of delusion and suffering, starts in the mind with fundamental ignorance—not knowing the difference between mental creation and reality. In other words, that fundamental ignorance deludes the mind into perceiving mind's creation or projection as reality. Therefore, if we want to find freedom from samsara, logically we need to go to its very root. As long as the root is not challenged, samsara will continue, no matter how much effort we exert to transcend it. By following the inquiries taught in the Dzogchen tradition, we arrive at the liberating realization that even mind itself is not so solid. This realization can lead to the collapse of the foundation of samsara, which is ultimately a creation of our own mind.

In the realm of such realization, we can see the illusory nature not only of samsara but of mind itself. This realization comes with an authentic experience of being liberated. It is not just a theory but a truth that we can literally live. It is like watching a movie in a dream, where the movie, the screen, the projector, and projectionist are all part of the dream. None of them are real.

The Four Establishments

Generally speaking, in Vajrayana and especially in Dzogchen, there are stages of "establishments." The first is establishing appearances as mind. This is coming to an understanding, either theoretically or experientially, that everything one is experiencing or perceiving is not real but is just a display of one's own mind. There are many similes, reasonings, and methodology that allow us to see this truth.

The second establishment is that mind, the source of our sense of reality, is also not so real and is empty, devoid of any intrinsic solidity. It is ungraspable. One cannot find its location because it lives in the border between existent and nonexistent. This is called establishing mind as empty.

That is not the end of the establishments because it could be a dead-end if we think there is nothing. We could fall into subtle nihilism. Therefore, to counter such a possibility, the next stage is establishing emptiness as awareness. Rather than getting stuck with emptiness as only mental negation, this stage puts life into it.

The last stage is establishing the union of awareness and emptiness, which is the complete integration of all the establishments. There is nothing further to be realized about the nature of mind, and all is balanced. All the three previous establishments are fully integrated with each other. Such understanding is no longer subject to any kind of intellectual mistakes such as eternalism or nihilism. One reason for this fourth establishment is so that one's mind does not get stuck holding on to any one of those three establishments. Instead, in the last stage, we hold onto all three establishments simultaneously. That is the complete realization of the ultimate truth, without lacking anything.

These four establishments show the importance of understanding the nature of mind. It shows that all our experiences, even right now in this very moment, are a display of our own mind, whether we are feeling happy or experiencing a struggle, seeing good or seeing bad. They are all a projection of mind. This mind itself is also not as solid and real as we think it is. Therefore, the good news is that the root of samsara is built on very shaky ground. With continuous inquiry, we find that not only is the mind not solid and without intrinsic nature, but also, in not finding anything to hold onto as mind, the nature of mind is revealed as pure awareness, the dharmakaya mind.

Collapsing the Shed of the Mind

This verse is a meditation on what is known in Dzogchen writings as "collapsing the shed of the mind." This analogy speaks volumes. In Tibet, a shed is common; it is a small house, a hut. Unlike an indestructible citadel that is heavily fortified, a shed is rather flimsy and does not stand on any foundation. It is quite easy for it to collapse. The simile is that the mind too is easily collapsed.

This seems contrary to our normal experience of everyday life, in which the mind appears to be so solid, especially when we get lost in thoughts and emotions. Our sense of reality—here and there, this and that, good and bad, success and failure, you and me—seems to be so real. But it is literally a construct of our own mind, and with powerful inquiry, the whole thing can collapse right in front of us. It is like the moment in the story *Alice in Wonderland* when Alice looks at the queen and says, "You are nothing but a pack of cards!" at which point the entire scene collapses, and Alice wakes up from her dream.

If you look at Alice's dialogue from a Buddhist point of view, it has wisdom. Even though the queen looked powerful and majestic, she was not as she appeared, and everything was just literally a pack of cards ready to collapse. Somehow Alice was able to see the illusory nature of that majesty, and through that insight, the queen was doomed to collapse.

Similarly, the very notion of reality that we unquestionably believe to be true is just like the queen. And like the queen was just built out of cards, this reality is just built out of our mind, thoughts, belief systems, and perceptions. Knowing this can bring about a very powerful paradigm shift in understanding reality and will lead us to understanding the mind itself.

The mind itself is groundless, has no foundation, is nowhere to be found, and can morph from one state to another. It is unreal yet at the same time, it is not nonexistent, otherwise we wouldn't be experiencing it. It is a mystery, not to be scared of but to be enjoyed completely.

Inquiry

The guidance on the actual inquiry begins by inviting you to turn your attention inward to examine what is chief among your body, mind, and speech; that is, to find out what is in charge of all the activities in your life.

In Buddhism, we say that mind is the forerunner of all our activities. This is quite obvious in our everyday life. For example, everything we do is motivated by some thought or intention, such as the simplest things in our daily life—going for a walk, making a cup of tea, or having a conversation with a friend. And then, obviously, the bigger steps we take in our life—like changing our career or moving to another country—are all propelled by thought, intention, and motivation.

Mind is also the apparatus through which our body experiences being alive. Imagine that your body is like a car or other vehicle, and your mind is the driver. A car doesn't drive by itself; at least in the past it didn't. You are holding onto the wheel and directing the vehicle.

This inquiry leads to an important insight. We come to the realization that everything in our life is directed by our mind. Therefore it is essential to pay attention to what the mind is and to understand it. In that sense, you can say that mind is chief among body and speech since they are both directed by the mind. This is why more advanced teachings in Buddhism tend to focus on discipline or spiritual practice in relation to the mind rather than in regards to words and actions. Although, of course, in all Buddhist systems, everyone is also encouraged to practice wholesome deeds through words and actions, and to avoid unwholesome deeds.

This emphasis on the mind is depicted not only in classical texts but through famous anecdotes, such as the dialogue between the *geshes* (W. *dge bshes*), or scholars, and the Tibetan yogi Milarepa. One time, after Milarepa became popular, a lot of doubt arose in the minds of the geshes, questioning who he was, what he was teaching, and his understanding of Buddhist doctrine. The scholars had a rigid idea that to truly understand Buddhism, you had to understand doctrines such as Vinaya. They asked Milarepa, "What is Vinaya?" to challenge and test him. They thought he would most likely fail. Milarepa simply replied in a song, with a little bit of sarcasm:

I don't know the Dharma so-called-Vinaya, Vinaya
If you tame your unruly mind, that's the Vinaya.

The etymology of the word *Vinaya* in Tibetan is *dulwa* (W. *'dul ba*), which means taming. Vinaya, one of the main Buddhist treatises, contains the entire monastic system of precepts to be observed by monks and nuns. It doesn't deal so much with what to do with your mind but more with words and especially actions. The precepts can be very detailed, including how to eat and so forth. In his song, Milarepa says that the true Vinaya is not about understanding the Vinaya system but is looking inside and taming your mind. Mind is the most important component to take care of—even more than actions because all your actions follow your mind.

In the verse we are examining, mind is called chief among the three gates (body, speech, and mind), meaning that all our actions are propelled by our mind, and mind is the very apparatus that gives rise to all our experiences, as if it is the creator of reality. So in the text, the mind is referred to as the all-creating king. This term is mostly mentioned in Dzogchen Tantras and has to be interpreted in that context.

The next step in the inquiry process is to find out what this mind is all about—whether it is real or not, whether it has solid ground or not. In this inquiry, we begin to look into our mind. This inquiry can be quite detailed—does mind have form? size? shape? color? This may sound like an unusual inquiry to some people. We are already under the common impression that mind has none of these. But it is important to do this because when you look into your mind to find its characteristics and inquire into the nature of mind, there is an opening where you see the groundless nature of mind right there.

Preparation for Inquiry

Let's say you are ready to do this inquiry. You might like to start with a posture. In Dzogchen, posture is meant to bring about ease and relaxation in your body. When your body is relaxed, naturally your mind begins to feel ease, without strife or struggle. This turns out to be a very important point, something that meditators should not miss.

Usually, the posture is sitting cross-legged on a comfortable seat or cushion with your back straight. You might like to rest your hands on your knees, which is called *sem nyid ngel sö chak gya* (W. *sems nyid ngal gso'i phyag rgya*), resting in the nature of mind. There is a saying that if the right auspicious conditions occur in the body, then realization comes into being naturally.

Here, *right auspicious conditions* means the right posture. It is saying that if you just take the right posture, then awakening, insight, peace, calmness, whatever you are looking for, will happen naturally. It is giving a hint that you don't need to struggle to achieve any of them.

The place could be outdoors or indoors. It seems that in the old days, many people meditated outside. It doesn't really matter where you meditate. Your home could be a perfect temple. Wherever you are meditating is a true temple even if it doesn't have a beautiful roof or sacred images. Often, not only the Dzogchen tradition but all Buddhist traditions emphasize the right or ideal conducive place to meditate, such as in the forest, in the wilderness, in solitude, or in a temple. It is not that these places are more sacred than anywhere else, such as our own home. Rather, these places provide a quiet environment where all our usual activities can be put on hold, and there are no unrelated activities happening there. Even if other people are there, they may also be engaging with meditation, contemplation, and so forth, under specific guidelines.

Therefore, in the sutras and many other writings, the right place is exalted. This is clearly seen in Longchenpa's famous poem, *Song of the Wildwoods,* in which he praises the wildwoods as the ideal place to live in order to fully immerse oneself in Dharma practice. All the great Dzogchen masters, like Shabkar, Patrul Rinpoche, and Longchenpa, spent a great deal of time in the wilderness. Their time in the wilderness played a critical role in their profound awakening.

If a meditator is distracted without knowing it, it can be difficult to immerse themselves single-pointedly into inquiry. There is a big difference between practicing with complete focus or with half-hearted focus. This may be true not just for spiritual practice but for everything else we do in our life. But going to a specific place is just a suggestion; it is not mandatory. As long as the meditator is able to take time away and has the capacity to get into inquiry completely with their whole being, then the place could be anywhere.

In accordance with the Dzogchen tradition, meditation starts with reciting a sacred liturgy that invokes what is called "the blessing of the lineage." This can be a very powerful method for transforming your mind. There are numerous lineage prayers. Reciting a lineage prayer that you have a connection with or an affinity to would be most appropriate. Lineage prayers often consist of hymns to the masters of the lineage, such as Padmasambhava and Yeshe Tsogyal. Lineage prayers are more than just hymns or supplications to the noble masters. You are also praying that you might realize the nature of your mind, or be awakened. You are mentally conjuring up their enlightened mind, which already gives you a pointer to the nature of mind that you want to experience, because these Dzogchen masters are the embodiment of awakening.

Reciting a lineage prayer is a powerful tool because it generates the sense that we are deeply connected with the lineage in which we are practicing the inquiry. It also validates that our practice is part of a tradition with a history of carrying the blessing, or liberating potency, that served as a vehicle for the awakening of many in the past. As we said, the lineage masters represent the embodiment of the enlightened mind we are seeking, so praying to them can invoke the sense that we are moving toward that same enlightened state. Sometimes we can feel that we are experiencing the enlightened mind that they represent. Offering lineage prayers is also a form of surrender, where we let go of our ego and our resistance. Our resistance to awakening can take many forms that are not always palpable. But the lineage prayer can help us to drop all of them. If resistance is frozen in our heart, this will melt it.

Reciting Dzogchen *dohas* or short Dzogchen liturgies to start the meditation is also conducive to practice. They become like meditation guidance or reminders to yourself. It seems that our mind gets a lot of benefit from reminders. Meditation guidance is reminding us to be fully present to see the nature of mind. Even though we might feel that we already know the nature of mind, without such a precise reminder, forgetfulness sneaks in, and there is a possibility of forgetting what we are supposed to be doing while we are meditating.

Meditation itself is quite diverse and has many forms. Some types of meditation are regarded as mundane meditation, which is meditation that doesn't really help you become enlightened. It may help you to find some temporary mental peace or release some emotional pain, but it doesn't help you develop compassion or be awakened to the ultimate truth.

One time, it is said that Gampopa reported to his teacher Milarepa that he was able to stay in a meditation that lasted for seven days. Not only that, he said that many Kadampa practitioners regarded this state of mind in meditation as exalted. Milarepa started laughing hysterically and chastised Gampopa, pointing out that this kind of meditation was just the fourth *jhana*, which was still considered worldly meditation, lacking the power of awakening to the nature of mind. Many Dzogchen masters often warn us not to be easily satisfied with our meditation because while we may love our meditation, it could just be a beautiful state of mind that we are reveling in, with temporary peace but without the power to shake the ground of samsara.

Recognize The Mind

Once you have prepared to meditate, perhaps the first thing you have to do is energetically turn your attention to look at your mind. Sometimes *mind* can sound abstract. Here we are not speaking of mind in general as some kind of abstract, philosophical topic. We need to see mind right here. We can do it by looking at who is thinking in this moment, or who is hearing. The one who is thinking, hearing, feeling, and sensing right now is the mind in this moment. Whatever is happening in the moment—that which is aware of it is the mind. Therefore, mind is not some big, grand, distant phenomenon that needs to be philosophized about or that requires a great deal of effort to find.

Mind is, in some sense, the most obvious and most available phenomenon. When we invoke our philosophical impulse, we may have doubts about the whole reality, including houses, roads, electric poles, and so forth. Sometimes we may wonder if everything is a dream, illusion, or projection of our mind. But one thing we can be sure of is that there is mind. We don't have to go anywhere to find mind. Whether one is thinking about what mind might be, or doubting reality, or coming from a materialistic point of view, thinking only physical reality exists, all these thought processes are happening in mind. So mind is the most obvious thing.

This is why when the Western philosopher Rene Descartes was lost in deep inquiry into the nature of reality, he came to the conclusion that he was real because he was able to think. He said, "I think therefore I am." He used the mind as immediately available proof that he existed. Of course, Buddhists might use the reverse logic, using mind's thought process to prove that self is not real. They might say, "I think, therefore I am not." The point is, whether we use mind to prove things are real or not, mind is always there. It's not that we have to figure it out. The one who is thinking and feeling right now is mind.

For example, just pause right now and see what is happening in your foot. You might feel the sensation that it is touching the ground. Who is feeling that? It is the mind. Or look up and see a cloud drifting. Who is seeing that? It is the mind seeing that the world is alive. So to look into the mind is to look into the mind that you can recognize right now.

Three-Part Inquiry

Once you see the mind, then you continue the inquiry by analyzing three points: Where does mind come from? Where is mind located? And where does mind go? The object of this inquiry is mind but mind can also refer to all of our experiences.

Where does the mind come from? This inquiry can be quite improvisational. You can say it doesn't come from outside, it doesn't come from any elements, etc. You will not find, of course, any origin of the mind outside itself. Then you can see if the mind has an origin within you. You can look for the origin of mind in your body, in your organs, or in mind itself. In the end, you'll come to an authentic, visceral recognition that there is no particular place that the mind comes from. When you don't find anything, you can let yourself rest in that not-finding the origin of mind.

The second part of this inquiry is to look for where the mind is located. You can look around and see if there is any place outside yourself where it could be located, such as in the elements. Then you might look for where mind is located inside, searching for any particular location or residence, such as in your body, in your organs, or in mind itself. When such inquiry results in the visceral understanding that there is no particular location of mind, you might like to rest in that not-finding.

The third part of the inquiry is to look for where the mind goes away. Some people may have a hard time relating to this notion. But you could look at a thought or emotion—they go away on their own. Then you can ask, where did they go? Did they go outside into the elements or go into your system? The inquiry is similar to the first two and will result in the visceral, intuitive recognition that there is no particular place inside you where the mind goes. When you cannot find the destination of the mind, then rest in that not-finding.

Wisdom of Not Finding

"Not-finding" here is like the essential wisdom, or *prajna*. Prajna is the very means that can liberate our mind by seeing the ultimate truth. In that sense, wisdom is praised as the ultimate virtue in all Buddhist teachings. This is true in Dzogchen as well. For example, the Adibuddha, or Samantabhadra, was enlightened, or awakened, not because of any virtues like holy deeds, recitation, and so forth, but simply by the power of wisdom. The logic behind this is that all of samsara starts from ignorance, or delusion, and not from any type of original sin, impurity, or negative karma. Such ignorance is not seeing the true nature of one's mind or reality. In that sense, samsara is the creation of such unawareness. Therefore, enlightenment comes from the power of wisdom to dispel this inner veil.

The pure nature of mind is luminous and can never be conditioned by anything. Nothing can change its nature. It can only be veiled temporarily by incidental conditions. There is no original fault in it. But unawareness or ignorance can veil this pure nature of mind, and we can be lost in a dreamlike world of delusion. No need to quote a grand mythology or parable—even a simple folk story like the *Ugly Duckling* can describe this situation. The ugly duckling was convinced that she was an ugly duckling and felt quite bad. She felt that she didn't belong to any species and was an outcast. Then one day she looked in the lake and saw that she was a beautiful swan. This is usually a story told to children, but it carries a great message, one which all nondual traditions are trying to express. The ugly duckling was always a swan. There was not one single moment that she was an ugly duckling. She was born as a swan but out of ignorance, she didn't realize who she was, and she suffered. There was nothing wrong with her originally. It's not like she was an ugly duckling that became a swan. This story can be used to describe how forgetfulness causes us to descend into samsara, because we are not remembering or not knowing the luminous nature of our consciousness.

Wisdom, or prajna in this context, has an aspect of deconstructing; in this case, deconstructing any kind of solidity for our mind. Such wisdom can be a little bit paradoxical. Sometimes wisdom is so heavy in our collective imagination, associated with finding or knowing something. In this case, wisdom is undoing, unlearning, and not finding. Therefore, a saying quoted by many masters is, "Not finding is the greatest finding." In one of his verses, Shabkar, the great Dzogchen master of the nineteenth century, said,

> *How amazing. Once again, my fortunate disciples,*
> *listen to me:*
> *While you investigate and analyze in such a way,*
> *you will not find a thing that you can point a finger at and*
> *say, "This is mind,"*
> *not even something that truly exists, even as a speck of*
> *dust or particle.*
> *That not-finding is the supreme finding.*

This not-finding is more than merely a theoretical understanding of the nature of mind but is accompanied by a deep feeling of being liberated, even though no major shift is happening in the external conditions of one's life. A true joy arrives in such a moment as the underlying suffering, which comes from holding everything to be so real and solid, dissolves. It resembles the moment when a chain or shackle has finally been removed from one's body. Most of the time, our struggles in life come from solidifying reality. We hardly question whether life is built upon the countless projections and perceptions of our mind. This inquiry invites us to stop solidifying reality for a while and look inside to realize that mind is making up all kinds of stories that we perceive as reality. We see that mind itself is no longer solid and we can experience the collapse of all our struggles and suffering.

One expression for *the world* in Buddhism is the "prison of samsara." This is not to say that this world is literally a prison but that the state of mind for most people is like a prison of kleshas. *Klesha* is perhaps the most important Buddhist psychological term to understand. The literal meaning of it is inner defilement, such as greed, hatred, and ignorance.

In the West, some teachers translate *klesha* as neurosis, which may not be an accurate translation but it is a shocking and creative one. If someone tells you that you are full of defilements, it might sound too abstract. But if someone tells you that you are full of neuroses, that will get your attention. You could be offended, or you might ask yourself if it is true or not. Buddhism teaches that not just a few individuals are filled with kleshas but that all of humanity is engulfed by them. It is not an individual situation but a collective one. This fact is pointed out not only by spiritual masters; there is a common realization among many people today that this human world is not as sane as one wishes it to be.

One time at a dinner party at someone's home in Minneapolis, a city in the United States, someone wore a T-shirt with a caption that said, "Welcome to Earth, the mental asylum of the universe." Somehow, that really cracked me up. I should have been saddened instead of laughing at this caption, but there is humor in pointing out the rampant craziness that seems to be the general state of mind. It is a humorous image but also partly the truth, and when you combine that message with a wild image, it is hard not to laugh.

In general, human suffering springs from holding on and making things real. But when we turn inside and truly inquire, often our version of reality is a mental construct; and when we look into our mind, our mind is also insubstantial and lacking any intrinsic nature. Such contemplation will create a crack in our version of reality sooner or later.

Trekchöd: Cutting Through

So the good news is that you can more or less let go of anything because mind is not so solid from the very beginning. This not-finding not only allows us to savor the taste of inner freedom but will lead us to an epiphany by seeing the unconditioned nature of who we are and the unconditioned nature of mind. Such an epiphany is at the heart of *trekchöd* (W. *khregs chod*), which is one of the two systems of Dzogchen along with *tögal* (W. *thod rgal*).

The literal meaning of *trekchöd* is cutting through immediately, right away. This system is described as a radical way to cut through dualism, or our tendency to reify. It is often described as the effortless path of the lazy ones because it does not require any further techniques other than simply seeing the nature of mind on the spot, which cuts through all dualism. For now, this is a simple way of defining *trekchöd* rather than other more elaborate definitions. There are more details later in this book.

One could instantaneously enter the path of no-ground and no-root.
Otherwise, they rest naturally within the pure space [of the mind].
They will enter the path of the ultimate secret within three weeks.
For those with lesser capacity,

Point out the two states of stillness and movement.
Taking the mind as the path leads to the
expanse of awareness.

Even though everyone has inherent buddha nature—from that point of view, everyone is the same and equal—there is another dimension, which is one's individuality, and from that point of view, we are all different. This is an obvious truth that does not require any logic. Even our forms, or physical appearances, are quite unique. This is not to say that some are better than others. But we are quite different, and this is also true regarding our mental makeup, deep-seated inclinations, and even our capacities. But remember, these are not permanent traits. They can change and evolve. Some people may have an inclination for certain paths and practices, and some have a sharper mind and more readiness to wake up. This is a reality in life.

Imagine that a host of individuals begin to practice the Dharma—some would understand wisdom faster and would even go through transformation more quickly than others. When Buddha taught, there was an entire sangha around him who followed his teachings. Some of them actually woke up, and they were called *arhats*. Even though all the people listened to the same master, the speed of their inner transformation was contingent on individual factors.

Based on observing how people make progress on the spiritual path, the category of three types of individuals was established: those with highest capacity, those with medium capacity, and those with lowest capacity. Within these three categories, of course, there could be subcategories. Since the system of categories was based on direct observation of how people evolve, it is not some unfounded theory.

Willingness and Devotion

These categories should not be interpreted as a kind of judgement or convey any sense of prejudice, because all these internal conditions can be changed if one has willingness. These categories often have to do with the willingness to wake up more than anything else. Someone could have extraordinary intellectual capacity and outward diligence but if there is no real willingness to wake up, then inner transformation does not come that easily.

This reminds me of the story of the monk who had dozens of students. All of his students became arhats or enlightened ones. As a result they gained clairvoyance and saw that their master was not enlightened. So they decided to repay his kindness by trying to enlighten him. Some of them encouraged him to practice in order to become enlightened, and in the beginning he resisted. Eventually his heart opened, and he also became an arhat. This illustrates that someone can be extremely intelligent—so much so that their role is guru or spiritual master—and can demonstrate outward spiritual discipline and practice but can lack true inner willingness to be enlightened.

Bear in mind that these three categories are not a measurement of some type of spiritual IQ or basic intelligence. This capacity is really determined by the level of devotion one has to enlightenment or the highest truth. Such sincere devotion will bring about awakening in anyone's consciousness. There are numerous anecdotes about panditas, or erudite scholars, such as Naropa from Nalanda University, who couldn't become enlightened despite all the knowledge he had gathered from the scriptures. In the end, Naropa had to leave his monastery to find someone who could wake him up. These ancient anecdotes are continually reminding us that devotion is the key ingredient for enlightenment.

Devotion is part of life in general, not only just in the spiritual sense. Devotion is a form of dedication: dedicating yourself to something—a cause, a relationship, an ideal. It is usually not contrived. There is authenticity because you are attending to or loving something with sincerity from the bottom of your heart. It also has the quality of surrender, in which you are willing to let go of some powerful attachment, which could be anything...attachment to concepts, or even attachment to self.

No Ground, No Root

This verse is stating that the individual with the highest capacity will be able to be liberated right away in an immediate fashion, simply by entering the path of instantaneous awakening, in which one realizes the nature of mind that has no ground and no root, *zhi mé tsa drel* (W. *gzhi med rtsa bral*). There are many historical figures who belonged to this category of individuals with the highest capacity. With individuals in this category, the inner awakening can happen in an immediate fashion, without any kind of lengthy struggle and without going through the usual process. That awakening is not considered an intellectual understanding but is a direct experience of the true nature of reality, which comes with the power to purify many of one's karmic patterns.

No ground, no root is one of the most essential terms in Dzogchen. Words can sometimes be insufficient in relation to what they are trying to convey. The term *no ground, no root* obviously has negation in it. It is negating any kind of solid ground or root for our mind. But in the end, it is not really negation. It goes beyond the logical language of affirmation and negation. It becomes another name for the absolute nature of reality, which can never be captured in any logical or rational terms. In simple language, it is about not finding any solid phenomena supporting our mind. Through the inquiry described earlier, *no ground, no root* is something that a person can experience directly rather than being a conceptual presentation of the nature of reality.

In the hierarchy of capacities, below those at the highest level are those with medium capacities. Somehow, due to their lacking the right circumstances or inner readiness, unlike the first individuals, these individuals will go through some process in order to be awakened.

In this verse, it is said that those with medium capacity will enter the "path of the ultimate secret," which refers to Dzogchen, by meditating on the nature of mind for three weeks. *Nature of mind* here is referred to as pure space, which describes the nature of mind that is unconditioned, indescribable, naturally free from all kleshas, and beyond birth and death. The characteristics of these individuals is that they might not be ready to awaken right away, but after the process of meditating for three weeks on the nature of mind, they will be awakened to true rigpa.

In some sense, even though there are three kinds of individuals with quite different abilities, in this context even those with medium capacity can come to an experiential understanding of the nature of mind within a relatively short period of time. This is due to two factors coming together: such an individual has a certain level of capacity, and the individual is applying a very powerful means for awakening. If the individual with this capacity is practicing under the umbrella of Dzogchen, and the individual has an epiphany in three weeks, the main catalyst is the method he or she is using. Not only is the practice profound, but having a skilled master or guide will make a huge difference.

Stillness, Movement, and Awareness

Individuals with lesser capacity may not be ready to be awakened right away, or even in a short period of time. Yet they can distinguish the two states of mind, *né* (W. *gnas*) and *gyu* (W. *'gyu*), stillness and movement. The first one, *né,* is abiding, which is a meditative state of mind where the mind becomes very still, without too much mental activity. It is often compared to a calm sea without waves. The second one, *gyu wa*, is a mind with mental activities, such as thoughts of past, future, and present, as well as the emotions that accompany thoughts. The term *né-gyu* is often used in traditional meditation instructions. It doesn't take a long time for a meditator to reach and recognize these mental states experientially.

There are numerous instructions on how to recognize these mental states. For example, while you are meditating, if you look into your mind, if your mind is still and calm, that state is *né*, abiding. And if your mind is active or thoughts are occurring, that is *gyu wa,* movement. Often, the term *rig* comes after *né-gyu,* such as *né-gyu-rig*. *Rig* refers to awareness and in this context it means the state of mind that is aware and recognizes whether the mind is in movement or stillness. These three states are easy to identify. Let's say you are meditating. If you remember to pause and see what is happening in your mind, the state that recognizes what is happening—stillness or movement—is awareness in this context.

Awareness can be interpreted in different ways, so remember not to get attached to one definition of it. In general, the term *awareness* is very big and can refer to something such as mindfulness all the way to buddha mind, the egoless state of mind. In the end, this term has to be understood in the context that one is working in.

Awareness—recognizing your state of mind—is an important step in our meditation practice. It helps us not to identify with our experiences, and it can also lead us to a profound realization of the enlightened nature of our mind, or to experience the egoless state of mind. In some sense, this experience sounds very simple, but its effect is extraordinary because in ordinary life we are lost in our thoughts and experiences all the time. Through such unawareness, samsara is continuously turning like a vicious circle of delusion in our consciousness. It becomes the only reality that there is, which is why we use the expression *wandering in samsara.* This is the opposite of awareness. It can be named ignorance, or unawareness, yet it is hard for us to accept that we are always living under the control of unawareness. It is a difficult truth to accept, and perhaps the true spiritual path begins when we are able to humbly accept this.

The simple contemplative practice of recognizing stillness and movement will help us immediately to step away from the vortex of unawareness so we are no longer unconsciously lost in our mind. This often comes with a feeling of being liberated. This contemplation is not about trying to be in stillness versus movement or in movement versus stillness. It is about not being bogged down in your mind but staying present as a witness. The ultimate goal of this contemplation in Dzogchen is to eventually transcend even these categories of stillness and movement, realizing that they are the same in their essence. They are simply a display of pure awareness itself. This realization can change our life completely from within.

In the beginning, meditators can intentionally turn their mind within to recognize which of these two states their mind is in. At some point, it is not even necessary to do such an inquiry. Once one's meditative awareness has matured, the two states become the same, in the sense that one is not better than the other, and it is not necessary to label either state. This maturity comes with the ability to stay in awareness regardless of what is happening in one's mind. Even awareness will mature, and it will be more than the ability to be aware of what is happening. It will evolve into a transcendent awareness, a non-egoic state of consciousness, or the dharmakaya mind.

First, single-pointed mind on the two as one.
Then, resting without looking, the potential energy of mind itself manifests.
Empty, suddenly wakeful, all thoughts remain empty and unrestrained.
Remaining in empty clarity is called self-illuminated mindfulness.
The first two actualize whatever arises.
The latter two, through their mode of apprehension,
Remain in no-thought, where all mental activity has ceased.

In essence, these lines are summarizing four categories or variations of the way we practice mindfulness.

The first one is that initially, the meditator distinguishes between abiding (stillness) and movement. Then at some point, that inquiry is no longer needed. Instead, in one's awareness, the two states become the same, without even the slightest preference. Then one remains single-pointedly in that awareness,.

The second one is that, without looking at or engaging with thoughts, leave the mind alone as it is. Whatever arises, which is the display of *tsal*, the potential energy of awareness itself, is clearly seen by that very awareness. Yet there is no more grasping onto any forms and thoughts that arise within the field of awareness.

The third one is remaining in a state where coarse and subtle mental activities are no longer operating, including our usual daily thoughts and moods, as well as thoughts that we might label as spiritual. They are all gone. It is like being shocked. When we are shocked, there is no longer any thought. The mind stops.

The fourth one is slightly different from the third one. Even though there are not so many coarse mental activities operating as there are in the usual state of our mind, there is also no clear awareness or ability to recognize or label one's experiences as this or that. There is only a subtle awareness. Awareness is aware of itself but not of anything beyond that. Remaining in that state is the fourth category.

These four categories are pointing out the different ways of practicing meditation. These differences come from using different techniques, and sometimes one method works better for someone at a certain time. But in the end, they are all doorways to the same awareness.

This verse is also pointing out that there is a demarcation between the first two ways and the last two ways: the first two completely welcome and embrace all the thoughts and mental activities that arise in the field of awareness as an expression or display of tsal, the potential energy of awareness. The second two are holding onto a reference point or staying in one particular state of mind, such as a thought-free state of mind, and having a preference for that state.

Shamata and Vipashyana

These four categories in some ways correspond to the standardized categories of meditation known as *shamata* and *vipashyana*. Although these two categories are ubiquitous across Buddhist traditions, the way they are practiced or defined can sometimes be very distinctive. This model of shamata and vipashyana is also used to describe the entirety of Dzogchen meditation.

In general, shamata refers to calmness and stillness, where at least the coarse mental activities subside. This state is induced by single-pointed concentration, or by blocking the senses and concentrating on a particular object, which might be breath, imagery, or sound. Shamata is quite similar in all traditions.

Whereas vipashyana is usually understood as the wisdom aspect of meditation, which is knowing something profound. Some Dzogchen masters said that shamata is like a person without faculties, hibernating in the cozy cradle of mindlessness whereas vipashyana is like a person with five sensory doors open wide.

Vipashyana means direct seeing. Direct seeing is more than conceptual understanding but knowing something experientially, as if *seeing* the truth through your senses. Vipashyana is taught in almost all Buddhist systems but with slightly different methodology and even different objectives.

Vipashyana in Dzogchen is typically described as effortless, spacious awareness, where all experiences—form, sounds, sights, touch, taste, and thoughts—are welcomed. This is often how people practice in the Dzogchen tradition. During meditation on rigpa, the meditator is encouraged to leave all the senses open, and welcome them in the field of one's own non-judging, non-grasping awareness. Just like the image of a person whose five senses are completely open, the meditator can hear, sense, touch, and feel.

All will have bliss, emptiness, and a variety of vivid appearances,
Which all can become objects of attachment and grasping.
In the body, speech, and mind, various experiences of discomfort and illness
Arise one after the other without any kind of ground.
Hope for and clinging to the good will arise;
Fear of the bad, seeing dangers as real, will arise.
All of these [experiences] cause one to become trapped on a narrow precipice of pitfalls and errors.

Meditation experiences often come with a variety of usual and sometimes unusual phenomena, which turn out to be the mind entertaining itself. Sometimes they can be quite pleasant and other times they can be unpleasant. Remember that mind is like a busy monkey, always restless and mischievous, playing pranks mainly on itself. It's like having a bad trip or a good trip, but it's all happening in your mind.

Bliss, emptiness, and no-thought are three common experiences that take place in Vajrayana meditation. Unusual visions may also arise. Many of these meditative states and visions may be very enticing, to such an extent that one could become hooked on them, and they become an obstacle. A good meditator can be so disciplined that nothing else can trap their mind, such as food or music or activities, but they could be still trapped by attachment to the meditative state. Just as a saying goes,

If a great meditator is not seduced by meditation itself,
Then nothing else will seduce her or him.

This saying has a lot of wisdom. It is not just something someone made up. Rather, it comes from the ancient wisdom of many generations of meditators. When we really immerse into meditative practices, we arrive at an amazing state where we are no longer attached to or distracted by worldly activities. This can feel very blissful, like we have transcended everything. But we can also be very attached to the wonderful experiences that come along with meditation.

But the "trip" may not always be good. It could be a very bad trip, where confusion, doubt, restlessness, and painful emotions can arise and be enhanced. If one is not aware, it is easy to get trapped by these experiences or want to avoid them. This is why we are reminded again and again in traditional teachings that we have to be aware of these phenomena when they arise. If we get attached to them, or scared of them, or have a preference, like hope and fear, the attachment becomes an obstacle to the path.

In addition, physical and emotional vicissitudes can occur to someone who is a great meditator, just as they do for anyone else. It is even possible that meditators may experience unusual situations or may feel everything more intensely than if they were living ordinary lives. This has to do with many things, including movement in their subtle body. Also, meditation can make someone hypersensitive, so that even small things become quite big in his or her experience.

The whole point here is not to be attached to any usual or unusual experiences and to welcome all conditions in the spirit of equanimity, not judging what is happening in a dualistic framework of wholesome or unwholesome, good or bad, right or wrong. It seems that many spiritual people can have quite deep-seated ideas about good and bad just like anyone else. But spiritual people also have ideas of wholesome or unwholesome, holy or profane, to the extent that they can take the form of superstition.

Generally speaking, unless there is a profound awakening, the human mind has an evolutionary, primitive tendency to perceive reality through the distorted lens of dualism. This comes with the belief that everything is intrinsically either good or bad. This is not to say that there is no good or bad. The problem is believing that things are intrinsically a certain way (which is not true and does not conform to the nature of reality). Vajrayana, Dzogchen, and Chöd are about transcending a dualistic perception. They do not deny mere appearance, or *nang tsam* (W. *snang tsam*) in Tibetan. *Nang* is appearances; *tsam* means just, or only. It sounds so simple on the surface, but this term is one of the most synthesized, cryptic terms to describe the nature of reality.

The ancient masters always say, "Do not negate nang tsam, mere appearances." What they are saying is that there are appearances, but that's all there is...things are appearing. Beyond that, even the idea of good or bad, beautiful or ugly, tree or mountain are just mental designations. Not just big things, like god or devil, but trees and pillows are mental designations. Of course, there are appearances, but our mind superimposes labels on them, dividing them into *this* and *that*.

This reminds me of an anecdote about two lamas hanging out together, looking at a tree. One lama points to the tree and says, "That thing is called a tree," and they both start laughing hysterically.

In the true meditative state, it is perhaps quite easy to realize that there are only appearances. All the labels and divisions of phenomena can dissolve, and there are only appearances. This is a moment when the veils of dualism dissolve. It is a moment when we can directly see the pure nature of all things. A profound understanding can arise. If the meditator remembers this moment and carries that wisdom throughout their life, relating to all situations from that nondual point of view, their heart will be freed from the pain of reactivity.

The all-encompassing, general outline, the essential point
of the path:
The three—happiness, suffering, and neutral—
all the experiences,
Definitively recognize them all as not truly existent,
Like false impressions of experiences.
Then relax without rejecting and accepting.
This [set of instructions] is the sole wisdom that
cuts through all pitfalls.

However one might identify oneself—meditator, yogi, Dharma practitioner—when the challenges mentioned in the previous verses arise, there is a panacea-like remedy. It's not that one needs to do certain spiritual practices, sadhanas, or mantras to deal with those challenges. From the Dzogchen point of view, all one needs to do is remember that all experiences—neutral, happiness, or sorrow—are not intrinsically real. They are just a display of one's own mind. Then remember to abide in equanimity where there is nothing to reject, nothing to hold onto.

Again, this is not denying the world of duality known as the relative truth. This is about knowing deeply the true nature of reality, which is called the ultimate truth. Then one can dwell in the world like anyone else, doing what others do—paying taxes on time, saving for retirement, working for political parties, or having preferences about diet. One will not be so lost in the web of dualism, knowing the whole thing is just a big drama or like the antics of a child building a sand castle.

If one is far away from a noble guide,
Then hold these five categories as the supreme path.
If one exerts too much effort in the practice single-pointedly,
Then the power of the mind will decrease, and only focused mindfulness becomes established.
While the body is human, the mind becomes like an animal's mind;
Some will be lost in mental instability.
Therefore, rely on a noble guide without separation.

The *kalyana mitra* is a noble guide or spiritual teacher for one who is on the path. The very notion of kalyana mitra was developed by Buddha himself, and there is a big emphasis on the benefit of having a spiritual guide across all Buddhist traditions. There are different levels of kalyana mitra. In Vajrayana or tantra, the teacher or kalyana mitra is more than a spiritual guide and even becomes one's guru.

Tibetan Buddhism often uses the term *noble master*, or *noble spiritual guide*. *Noble* implies that it is not enough to just have a spiritual teacher but to have someone who is noble, someone who has wisdom and compassion, someone who is not ruled by his or her own ego, someone who cares about the well-being of their students. This is the general description of a noble teacher or guide. A noble teacher is not trying to gain respect, admiration, and all kinds of benefits from the devotion of the disciple. It is, of course, always difficult to know who is enlightened or not, and who has wisdom, but it is said that if a teacher has authentic compassion toward the student and toward the world, then that teacher could be regarded as a noble teacher.

When it comes to the Vajrayana or Dzogchen system, the noble teacher has to be someone who is awakened inside, who has the skill and knowledge of how to help students. There will be setbacks, doubts, resistance, and pitfalls along the way. When these things happen, the master can help the meditator or Dharma practitioner overcome these obstacles and find clarity and light in the darkness.

Here, the verse is encouraging us not to be a long distance away from a spiritual guide. But it doesn't always mean physical distance; it can also be a metaphor. It is encouraging us to have a close connection with our own guru or master and work with him or her. The shortcoming of not having a close connection with a master is that we are left alone with our obstacles. When the obstacles manifest and there is no help, it is possible that we can be totally defeated by them and give up the path. Or the obstacle can take us into self-glorifying or grand delusions.

If one is not near a teacher physically, then the verse says to remember the five categories—the ability to recognize stillness and movement, and the four types of mindfulness described in the earlier verse. These categories become a compass guiding you through the practice when there is no teacher to consult with.

These four types of mindfulness are powerful steps toward the complete realization of rigpa, or luminous nature of mind. But one should not be attached to them; rather one should use them as methods. If one is attached to them and practices them too long with too much exertion, it can backfire. Then the method itself becomes bondage.

It's like someone crossing a river in a boat who is really attached to the boat and never gets out to reach the other shore but just stays in the boat paddling with all their strength forever. It can be quite exhausting and laborious if they continue to do that. Of course, the boat was needed in the beginning to reach the other shore, but it is important to remember it is just a means.

It is not hard for human beings to lose track and sometimes miss the whole point in all endeavors. All spiritual practices need to be done with moderation and balance. If that is lacking, it may mean one is attached to the practice itself. All attachment is a form of bondage, regardless of what the attachment is. It is always good to remember the advice spoken by Machig Labdron: "Do not be too loose, do not be too tight; that is the essential point of the view."

This verse is saying that if you are very attached to the four methods of mindfulness and you are practicing them with too much effort, then instead of giving rise to wisdom, they eventually dull your mind. This can even cause disturbance in your mind and subtle body as well. Therefore, it is always wise to check for signs of pitfalls while you are on the journey.

In brief, while taking mind as the path,
One is not even as close as a hair to the path of
liberation and omniscience.
Even if, for a long period of time,
One is practicing [in this way] with intense diligence,
Life would be squandered and wasted.
Understand this, fortunate ones.

All the meditative experiences described in these verses could be regarded as mundane, or worldly, meditation, which are lacking in the capacity to awaken our consciousness to the absolute truth. They are all simply nothing more than experiencing wonderful meditative states in the realm of unawakened, ordinary consciousness. For the most part, they are devoid of insight, or vipashyana, which is the direct seeing of the nature of mind.

This verse is also indicating that even though these meditative experiences have their own benefit as a doorway to transcendent meditation, they themselves are limited and would not take one to liberation. Therefore, the experiences are merely a stage of the whole journey that one might linger in for a while, but one would not stay there forever. They serve the practitioner at a certain level but at some point they are not of benefit if one is longing for true liberation.

For example, some meditation experiences are described as nothing more than being in *alaya*, or the basic ground, which is the experience of being peaceful and mindless, where all our usual mental activities are dormant. This is not a bad thing. Please remember that. This is part of the whole process and before one can be truly awakened, one may need to go through this sedentary mind experience. But one can stay in such a meditative state and not really get to the ultimate destination.

This is not hypothetical but happens in real life. In the contemporary world, meditation is widely practiced by many people from different walks of life, yet it does not mean that all meditation practices have wisdom, or prajna, as their essence. Such meditations may not lead to transcendence, but they can bring benefit like stress release and so forth. It is more like a spiritual band-aid, which has its own purpose.

If you are reading this book, you may not have to worry about this. You might be one of the "fortunate ones" that the Primordial Buddha is speaking to. Sometimes mistakes are part of the journey. They can often serve as a source of an entirely new wisdom. You are also not alone on this journey. There is always a guide who can help you find a way to return to the course.

These profound verses are already giving instructions on how to stay the course. They are like a guide that is always available when you call on them.

From the *Sharp Vajra of Awareness Tantra*, the first chapter on taking the impure mind as a path.

II. Direct Seeing

Actualizing the True Face of the Sharp Vajra

**When the sharp vajra of wisdom is actualized,
Awareness is exalted from the undifferentiated ground.
It is nothing whatsoever, beyond words, thoughts,
and description.
Without contrived meditation, nor accepting and
rejecting, naturally free,
It is spontaneously present as the sharp vajra of wisdom.**

This chapter is about Dzogchen vipashyana. It is said that all the meditation practices taught in the sutras and tantras fall under the umbrella of the shamata/vipashyana model—calm abiding and direct seeing into the nature of mind. True vipashyana in Dzogchen is the actual experience of awakening that comes with wisdom, or insight. All the Buddhist doctrines agree with each other that awakening can only happen in the realm of insight. The question is, what insight are we talking about?

It is said that everything that exists has two facades: one is what our ordinary mind perceives, and one is the way things are in actuality. This gives us the foundation for the two truths: the relative truth and the ultimate truth. But our mind does not easily see the true nature of reality, or the way things are in actuality. The mind is veiled by subtle unawareness that serves as the foundation or fuel that spins samsara, the wheel of unenlightened existence. Therefore, in order for samsara to be transcended, its genesis also has to be transcended. The genesis of samsara is unawareness, which in itself is not sin, bad karma, or vice. So unawareness is not regarded as bad by any means. But it can be a powerful basis for delusion or suffering when it governs consciousness.

The exact opposite of unawareness is wisdom. True wisdom is not about knowing anything in a conceptual way. It is simply that consciousness is no longer bound by unawareness. This is the ultimate way of defining wisdom in Dzogchen.

How does neutral unawareness become the cosmic genesis of samsara? Through unawareness, our mind creates an illusion of reality where things are separated into self and other, right and wrong, good and bad, nirvana and samsara. On the contrary, in the realm of ultimate truth, there is no duality, no separation between anything.

In the Dzogchen Tantras, the very singular factor for awakening is the power of wisdom, which is vipashyana. Remember that this is clearly said when the tantras describe the awakening of Buddha Samantabhadra. They say that Buddha Samantabhadra, the Primordial Buddha, became enlightened not through deliberately performing any kind of virtuous deeds. Nor had Buddha Samantabhadra done one single practice as a means of karmic purification. Buddha Samantabhadra became awakened through only one factor, which is this very wisdom, or prajna—the direct seeing into the nature of consciousness.

Two Accumulations

In general, Buddhism describes the factors for enlightenment as linear and systematic, such as in a relationship of cause and effect. Such a relationship involves time—cause comes before effect. Sometimes, there is also a doctrinaire assertion that two factors for enlightenment must be cultivated before full awakening to samyaksambuddhahood. These factors are called *punya sambhara* and *jnana sambhara,* or accumulation of merit and accumulation of wisdom. These two accumulations are not just abstract ideas but are described in a precise fashion. For example, out of the six *paramitas*, the first three—generosity, discipline, and endurance—are considered punya sambhara. The last two—meditation and transcendent wisdom—are considered jnana sambhara. The fourth, diligence, is considered the supporting basis for all of them because without diligence, one could not cultivate either punya sambhara or jnana sambhara.

This is a good system because it helps people practice Dharma in a complete way without any imbalance. For example, the practice of generosity is, of course, a powerful factor for enlightenment. But if there is no wisdom, then the practice of generosity would not lead one to authentic awakening. While practicing generosity and performing noble deeds, one could easily be caught in the snares of mistaken beliefs. Then one would be a spiritual, holy man or woman who is stuck half-way, going nowhere. This is convincing logic to show us that without wisdom, our spiritual practice could have limited power to fully set us free.

On the other hand, one could be focusing on meditation or transcendent wisdom, but there could be an imbalance where one is no longer paying attention to fundamental spiritual practices, such as discipline, generosity, and tolerance. From that point of view, the model of two accumulations is very helpful to everyone, functioning as a gauge to point out any deficiencies or imbalance in our spirituality. Sometimes the two accumulations can be regarded as the two wings of a bird. If one of them is missing, no matter how strong the bird might be, she would be unable to freely fly in the vast sky. This metaphor has truth to a certain degree when we hold this model of two accumulations.

Yet in the pure Dzogchen doctrine, the duality between these two accumulations is transcended. This does not mean that Dzogchen denies the need for these two accumulations as a factor for enlightenment. The solution for this, in regard to the awakening of Buddha Samantabhadra, who has done neither, is the interpretation that Buddha Samantabhadra's awakening is already the culmination of the two accumulations at the highest level. The fact that Buddha Samantabhadra didn't get trapped by any appearances or display of the mind is considered the perfection of the accumulation of merit. And the fact that Buddha Samantabhadra's mind is awakened to its true nature as pure luminosity can be regarded as the perfection of the accumulation of wisdom. Therefore, even though Buddha Samantabhadra has not done even one millisecond of accumulations, they are all completely perfect in such primordial awakening.

Vipashyana

Vipashyana is generally described as meditation that eventually leads to complete enlightenment. So vipashyana needs to be interpreted in context. In Dzogchen, it is a practice and sometimes it is more than that. Even the ultimate awakening is regarded as vipashyana because it has to do with seeing the unconditioned, pure nature of consciousness.

According to Dzogchen, awakening happens in the moment when consciousness is no longer remaining dormant in *zhi* (W. *gzhi*), or ground. Consciousness emerges from the ground by an incidental catalyst known as life force, *sok lung* (W. *srog rlung*). If consciousness realizes in that very moment its true nature as luminous, and that all appearances and experiences are merely its own display, then consciousness in that moment is fully enlightened. Such enlightenment is described in the instantaneous process of Buddha Samantabhadra's awakening. That very recognition—seeing everything as a display of consciousness itself—can be called vipashyana in this context because there is no truth higher than that. This is the very truth that liberates consciousness immediately. It is a totally nondual awakening because the seer and seen are the same. Consciousness is experiencing all these phenomena that are none other than itself and consciousness is also enlightened in that moment.

Perhaps the pivotal concept in the entire Dzogchen doctrine is ground, or zhi, which is the foundation of all phenomena, from which everything arises and upon which everything continues to play out. But that ground is also neutral because it is neither samsara nor nirvana, neither vice nor virtue, neither wholesome nor unwholesome. Ground itself is not awakened. If ground were awakened, there would not be any unawareness; there would be no ground upon which samsara could develop in the first place. In order for samsara to come into being, unawareness is required. Even though it is not samsara, ground remains in a neutral or undifferentiated state. Ground should not be defined as either enlightened or samsaric.

Yet through a powerful catalyst, *sok lung,* consciousness is "exalted" from the ground and begins to witness what is called *zhi nang* (W. *gzhi snang*), the display of ground, which is the phenomenal world. If in that moment, consciousness slips into ignorance, that leads to the samsaric development of delusions. But if consciousness somehow realizes that the whole phenomenal world is none other than its own display, consciousness is fully awakened in that moment. That awakening can be called enlightenment, buddhahood, Samantabhadra, or whatever you wish to call it.

View, meditation, conduct, ground, path, fruition,
Taking refuge, developing bodhicitta, six paramitas, deity, mantra, mandala—
They are all completely distilled into one essence within the sharp vajra.

This extraordinary awakening cannot be defined with any limitations. It is bigger than anything else that our mind can comprehend. Because of that, everything—all spiritual principles—is complete within that awakening. It is lacking in nothing. The very essence of all Dharmas and spiritual practices is completely contained in this awakening. Nothing is missing. The essence of all the variety of Dharma practices—taking refuge, developing bodhicitta, the six paramitas, the recitation of mantra, and so on—is perfect in that absolute awakening, without even doing any of them.

Let's try to make this whole thing more relatable to personal experience through Dzogchen terms: *ngowo* (W. *ngo bo*), or essence; *tsal* (W. *rtsal*), or dynamic energy; and *rol pa* (W. *rol pa*), or display. These three terms are quite approachable, and we can relate to them within our own experience.

The first term, *ngowo,* refers to the very essence, the pure, fundamental nature of our mind, which is empty. The very essence of mind is not a solid entity in any way. If we look for any realness or some kind of non-physical or metaphysical factors supporting the solidity of the mind, eventually we don't find even one speck of it. Not only is it lacking in any physical attributes such as form, shape, or size, it is also lacking in any mental ground that is solid enough to make it real or tangible.

Through inquiry, mind becomes the most mysterious phenomenon. It is obviously there, or none of us would be alive, thinking, or breathing. But it is not real, and we can never find what it is. In that sense, the essence of mind is empty. That emptiness is more than absence, but rather it turns out to be the most sacred of the sacred, so much so that it is often referred to as bodhicitta, enlightened mind.

The second term is *tsal*, potential energy, which refers to the state of mind that is present right now—vivid, the sense of being alive, alertness. Even with no thoughts, if you just sit, there is vivid, unhindered alertness. That is tsal, potential energy. The simplest way to find tsal is to just pause and be aware of the sense of being alive, being present, being alert. That can be identified as tsal. It is something we can access right now. Therefore, tsal is not a religious doctrine but an experiential term, which indicates that consciousness is not an abstract phenomenon but rather full of life.

While you are meditating, whenever you look into that alive, alert state of mind, where there is not much mental activity or movement, you can literally call that moment an experience of tsal. But remember, tsal is not some permanent state of mind where there are no more mental activities. Rather, because tsal is alive, nothing really hinders it. Therefore it is natural to have mental movement, thoughts, or emotions arise. If you forget that they are simply a display of your own consciousness and begin to reify them, then you are trapped in ignorance, or unawareness, caught by the spell of dualism. That state is called *rolpa* in this context.

If you just stay in tsal while welcoming all the myriad experiences from within or without, that is vipashyana. If you get swayed, that is rolpa.

Yet even this rolpa has a beautiful meaning. It is a sacred euphemism for delusion. Since rolpa also means miraculous display, even being deluded is a miraculous display. If you trace back the original delusion, it goes back to the pure luminous nature of mind, which in this context is bodhicitta. All our delusions come from that and will dissolve back into it.

In ordinary life, we see that the waves of the ocean are the display of the ocean, and the waves go back into the ocean. In the same way, all our experiences in this very life, whether beautiful, ugly, spiritual, secular, all come from that bodhicitta, and all our sorrow and suffering will dissolve back into bodhicitta. Our destination is nirvana—we have no choice!

As a reminder, the term *rolpa* does not always mean being caught up and deluded. It is only in this context of the three terms (ngowo, tsal, and rolpa) that it has that meaning. But it is a very useful term to apply in our life, either while meditating or while totally engaging with even menial activities. Because in all situations, we have the choice to pause and see what is happening inside us. In doing so, we always see that we are alive inside and outside, with our moods, emotions, thoughts, and our relationship to the world of form. We can simply recognize whatever is arising—sadness as sadness, fear as fear, boredom as boredom. That recognition will help keep us from descending into the trap of unawareness.

This recognition can sometimes sound too mechanical, like counting sheep. It can put you to sleep instead of waking you up. Instead, imagine that you are applying the term *rolpa*, and you are not only fully present and mindful of what is going on inside you and around you, not caught up in any one moment, and there is also joy or magic in the experience of witnessing. That joy is because you are welcoming whatever is going on, embracing it all as a miraculous display of something truly ineffable. When you open your heart, you can drink in everything as the pure nectar of life.

Then, [even though] controlled by the maras of unawareness and kleshas,
Sentient beings are realized in a single instant,
Omniscient perfect buddhahood is actualized,
And [they] become the field of merit for all beings, including gods.

Let's restate once again that such awakening is also the completion of all the Dharmas as well as the paths, and not even one Dharma is missed. The six paramitas (generosity, etc.) as well as the two stages of Vajrayana (creation and completion) are complete in this awakening. Through this awakening, all the karmic obscurations will dissolve in our consciousness. Nirvana, the absolute freedom, can be actualized in this very lifetime.

The higher tantras in Vajrayana as well as Dzogchen emphasize becoming fully enlightened in one lifetime. There is a radical theory in the Vajrayana Tantra that one can become enlightened in this very lifetime even if one has never entered the path in past lifetimes. It means that you can start from scratch and reach the highest freedom in a short period of time, whereas the systems in the sutras describe a lengthy process of enlightenment. For example, a Buddha needs to be on the path for three eons, which consists of many thousands of human lifetimes. After that, if all goes well, and Mara hasn't succeeded in creating mighty hindrances to disrupt the journey, then she or he will finally become enlightened after those three eons of walking the path. Whereas Vajrayana is considered the shortcut to enlightenment, and even among the Vajrayana paths, Dzogchen is considered the most dynamic and direct doorway to samyaksambuddhahood.

This logic is sometimes hard to believe in, but the true logic of such instantaneous awakening has to do with the fact that there is a pure state of our consciousness that has never been deluded and has never been bound by anything. This is called the luminous nature of mind. Seeing it has extraordinary power to dissolve even deep-seated habitual patterns and karmic tendencies that hold us back.

This powerful illumination is depicted through analogies, such as the darkness of many eons in a cave facing north that is dispelled in a single moment by the light of a flame. Such illumination is not purely a story or parable but an epiphany that many people went through and many will go through again and again.

From the *Sharp Vajra of Awareness Tantra*, the second chapter on direct seeing: actualizing the true face of the sharp vajra.

III. Actualization of the Ground Dharmakaya

The sharp vajra of discriminating awareness
Destroys the samsaric mountain of self-concept.
The root of samsara, self-grasping—
Analyze its origin, residence, destination as well as name and actuality,
Determining that it is objectless and empty.
This is the establishment of the selflessness of the individual.

No-self is the axis on which the entire Buddhist doctrine revolves. No-self is like the essential parameter for determining what is Buddhist doctrine and what is not, although there are various interpretations of no-self. This verse invokes a powerful image of the vajra wisdom of discernment destroying the mountain of self-concept. This image is also invoked by other Buddhist masters, and it is a traditional metaphor.

No-self is obviously a negation. You could say that all the philosophical assertions in Buddhism are either negation or affirmation. For example, the concept of all-pervasive sacredness in the tantras is obviously affirmation, and there is no obvious negation in that concept. But here, no-self is negation because it is negating the self.

Traditionally, it is said that there are two kinds of self: the doctrinaire self and the inborn, or co-emergent, self. The doctrinaire self is the notion of self that does not come naturally through birth but comes about when one is indoctrinated into a certain set of beliefs or philosophy. That self is more than just your visceral feeling of "I"; it is more cerebral. Whereas the co-emergent self is the sense of self in each of us that continues as a foundation of who we are. The clearest way to point it out is that if you say "I did that yesterday" or "I was born twenty or thirty years ago," there is a continuation of the sense of "I." There is a feeling that the "I" from twenty years ago and the "I" sitting here now are the same self. The sense of "I" is a feeling that develops on its own in the course of life from the earliest stages of our development. It is rooted in our consciousness and feels very visceral in that sense. It has nothing to do with philosophy.

While engaging in ordinary activities, the sense of "I am" continues to operate in our mind unless there is some kind of breakthrough where we see that the self is illusion. But often the sense of "I" is there like a background, a mental image of who we are. Then there are times that the sense of self becomes very strong and well-pronounced, whether we are elated or contracted. For example, if someone says, "You're great" or "You are this and that," there is a really strong sense of "I." Or if someone criticizes us, then the sense of self becomes pronounced, and we feel contracted in that moment. That is the co-emergent self because it comes simply from being human.

So the wisdom of no-self negates both versions of self: the co-emergent self as well as the doctrinaire self. Often the understanding of no-self is brought about by inquiry. In that sense, the wisdom of discernment can refer to inquiry itself as well as the experiential realization of no-self. Remember, this is negation, and even the image used implies negation. The vajra, the divine weapon, is destroying the mountain of concepts, which is a powerful analogy for negation, as the mental structure is ready to be dismantled, destroyed.

This also reminds us that self-concept is like a great mountain, majestic, powerful, rooted in our consciousness continuously, and serving as the very ground of samsara. Therefore, according to Buddhist doctrine, true liberation is not achieved by any virtuous deed but only through the realization of no-self.

The no-self expressed in this verse is specifically pointing out no-self of the individual. There are two categories of no-self, known as no-self of individual and no-self of phenomena. They are both the same as the notion of emptiness, or *sunyata*. In Mahayana, no-self is identical to the idea of emptiness.

We are living in a dream world most of the time, a world that is constructed out of thoughts, perceptions, and opinions. In a real dream, we usually experience everything we can do while we are awake—traveling, eating, visiting a city, or spending time with friends. In the dream, just like during the day, we could be feeling very strong emotions or having opinions. It is similar to the life that we think is real during the day. Theoretically you can dream about everything. Yet, none of these things in the dream are real —they are all happening in our mind.

There is a saying in the Golok region of Tibet that there is no limit to dreams except for two dreams: no one would dream of a bright sun, and no one would dream of a horse race in a tray. This is not to be taken literally, and we don't know if it is true or not. The point is that you could dream anything. The dream is the creator, full of infinite possibilities in its own dimension, just as the realm of life is during the day. There is a similarity between them. Many masters often use dream as a metaphor to point out that until we are truly awakened, we are living in a big dream, and the life that we think is true is mainly happening in our head, created by thoughts, concepts, and ideas.

There is even a genre of writing known as a debate between day and night reality. Lama Mipham wrote a well-known text on it, which is quite lively. He portrays day and night reality as two characters who have a philosophical debate about which one is real and which is unreal. They both present their best logic to prove that the other is not real. It is almost like putting emptiness in a play or dream to show that the very reality we are holding onto right now is not that real when it is questioned.

Sometimes even without contemplative inquiry, there are moments where something touches our consciousness and creates a crack in it. Then a spontaneous awakening happens which sees that the reality we believe to be true is nothing more than illusion. We see that there is a big reality, which is called emptiness, in which all the duality that our mind has been constructing—good, bad, self, other—is gone. It is not that one suddenly descends into a dark pit where nothing exists...it is hard to describe in language.

Often the reality which most people reify and grasp at turns out to be a giant dream spinning in their own heads. If it were fun, it would be okay to live in that world. But often it is not that much fun. It is a place where we get lost in conflicting emotional turmoil and trapped with erroneous concepts. There is a lot of needless pain in that version of reality.

The "vajra invitation" here is, through inquiry, to wake up from that dream-like reality and see the unconditioned, pure nature of reality, which is both profound and utterly simple. Even the name for the nature of reality can be both profound and very simple. Dharmata, the nature of all, is the profound name for it. Or it can be called suchness, *tathata*—such a simple word, which shows the simplicity of such truth. It can also be called by a technical, philosophical term, the selflessness of phenomena. All the names point to the same truth.

Seek the basis for labeling of self and object.
Determining that it is objectless and empty, then
Analyze how all things, all the way down to
partless particles,
Are lacking intrinsic nature and are empty.

Here is the inquiry that will lead one to awakening to no-self or great emptiness. This inquiry is often taught in other Buddhist teachings, but as a reader, you may feel there is a potency or blessing in the same inquiry in the context of this tantra we are studying.

Let's say you are about to meditate on no-self of phenomena, which means realizing there is no objective reality that has intrinsic nature in itself. You begin to inquire into an apple in front of you to see if there is an apple or not. Obviously, this would be quite interesting and radical because until that moment, you had no doubt that the object in front of you was an apple. Usually we don't question it; we just get to eat it, because it is delicious. So this is all a little peculiar. But for some reason, you question the whole concept of apple. Don't spend too much time on this because the apple could go bad in the meantime. But exactly what is an apple? Who decided to assert that this round thing in front of you is an apple, which is distinguished from everything else around it? Until this inquiry, there was a strong sense that it is an apple without any doubt, and it has particular characteristics. It is not a grain; it is a fruit. It is not passionfruit. It is not a banana.

Sooner or later, there will be an eye-opening realization that the object is no longer an apple. There is no apple. You realize that your mind and the mind of everyone else collectively superimposed a label on it. Not only that, the way you see the object itself is not what it is, especially if you begin to divide that apple into pieces, down to particles at the subatomic level. Then the whole thing turns out to be just a mental designation. There is not one single thing that is intrinsically apple. If you go down to the particles of anything, even the particles are questionable. It is simply the light or photons that are transmitted to receptors in our eyes, creating an image of an apple. This brings about the whole question of whether there is any kind of objective reality, even particles.

Do not worry that this inquiry will lead you into some kind of nihilistic nothingness. Even in this radical negation, we are not supposed to negate what are called "mere appearances," which means it is not about totally rejecting existence. Therefore, this inquiry can beautifully harmonize these two principles: there is no intrinsic nature of anything, yet there is existence.

Hopefully you will figure this out before the apple goes bad, and you can enjoy the apple completely. It will be delicious even though there is no apple.

Appearances of this life and the next life,
as well as dreams,
Are determined to be objectless within empty space.
Karmic cause and effect, virtue and vice, benefit from
gods, and harm from demons
Are all determined to be objectless and transparent.

All apparent existence, without any exception, including all the seeming reality of this life and beyond; including dreams and the whole world—all living beings, the five sensory experiences, and so on—are all devoid of inherent nature. Not only that, even the idea of karma or the law of cause and effect, the idea that good karma benefits us and negative karma harms us, the idea that gods are benevolent and demons are malevolent, the concepts of buddhas and buddha fields, and so on are all devoid of intrinsic nature. In deep inquiry, they all begin to collapse. They are all *trö pa* (W. *spros pa*), conceptual proliferation. In other words, they are simply mental constructs, which are layers of illusions superimposed on the true nature of reality.

There are two ways of reaching this radical insight, which we can call *nondual awakening*. One is through a series of inquiries. The practice of these inquiries is well-taught not only in Vajrayana but also in the general Mahayana Buddhist tradition. Even in Madhyamaka, the Middle Way, the inquiries bring about the realization that everything is not as real as it appears. For example, the works of Nagarjuna, Aryadeva, Chandrakirti, Shantideva, and many more have these inquiries. Sometimes the inquiries are very detailed and can sound very nitty-gritty. But they have the power to show us that things are not as real as we perceive them to be.

These traditional inquiries are very radical because they are not just questioning the intrinsic nature of mundane things but even things that are supposed to be extramundane. These inquiries eventually lead one to the radical realization that everything is emptiness, including the sacred. It seems that some of the early orthodox Buddhist schools didn't accept this; they thought it went too far. They thought that accepting the emptiness of things like buddhahood or nirvana was too nihilistic. But Mahayana masters extensively teach inquiries in which the intrinsic nature of even the most sacred is also questioned. In these inquiries, we realize that all reality—samsara, nirvana, gods, demons, and even the law of karma—is merely illusory, and none of it has any inherent truth, or svabhava.

This is not a nihilistic rejection. Everything has a role to play in relative truth, otherwise the world would not function. It's like fire—scientifically, it is broken down into gases and energy. But if you put your hand in fire, it will burn. Or a rock. Even a rock is not as real as it appears, but you need to treat it as a rock. Otherwise if you just run into it, it can cause a bruise or injury.

There is a famous anecdote about two monks who were sitting together chanting a puja for a family. The older monk was always trying to show off his knowledge and deep thinking.

While they were chanting, the younger monk was beating the drum with a stick, and the older monk paused while the younger monk continued drumming. After a long pause, the older monk said, "Where does that sound come from?" The question itself is a legitimate question, but the time was not the right time to ask it. The young monk knew this, so he took the stick and hit the old monk's head very hard. The old monk said, "Stop, that hurts me!" The young monk said, "Wherever that pain comes from, that's where the sound is coming from."

Just like that, you cannot deny anything. You have to respect everything in the relative truth, including the law of karma. It is a universal law. At the same time, this universal law needs to be transcended, otherwise you will be bound by duality forever.

But now another question is: how much do you have to pay attention to the law of karma in relation to your actions in the world? On one hand, karma is an illusion, like anything else. On the other hand, karma is as real as anything like a rock, a mountain, a drum stick, or the pain of being beaten by a drum stick.

The answer is that while keeping the big view of nonduality and emptiness in mind, we need to pay attention to the law of karma and apply it in our daily life. Otherwise, we could be fooling ourselves by using the idea of transcendence as an excuse to be careless with our actions in the world. Therefore, the Tibetan Buddhist masters say until the *namtok* (W. *rnam rtog*) are exhausted, one must respect the law of karma. *Namtok* literally means discursive concepts, but it is also a word for the inner poisons. Hypothetically speaking, if all your kleshas are exhausted, then you don't have to worry so much about what you are doing because your whole being is pure and free, and all your deeds and way of being become an expression of that purified state.

Buddhas and the buddha fields,
The objects of appearances and experiences of the three samsaric realms,
Determine that the ground and root of the three—origin, residence, destination—are non-existent.
All of them are objectless and empty.
Realize this meaning, not just by saying [the words].

Not only is our own life illusory and unreal but the whole universe is in some sense unreal, such as the three samsaric realms of form, desire, and formlessness. Even Buddha, buddhahood, and nirvana, which are the most sacred, are also illusions. Therefore on this path to nondual awakening, even they should be investigated with inquiry, which will result in the realization that they are as illusory as everything else.

Such inquiry will lead us to the realization that all notions of reality, ordinary or sublime, are just projections of our own mind. Nothing really exists as sacred or ordinary by itself. For example, there is the idea of *naraka* in many traditions, which is a realm where one experiences pure misery. However Mahayana, especially Vajrayana, teaches that the naraka realm is just a state of your own mind. On the other hand, the buddha field that is supposed to be the most sacred realm in the universe is also just a state of your own mind. When your mind is fully enlightened, the whole universe is actually a buddha field.

This is spoken again and again by true Vajrayana masters. Once Langri Thangpa, a well-known eleventh-century Kadampa master, said he failed with his prayer. He said he had been praying all along to go to hell so he could help all the souls in hell. But he came to an epiphany that there was no hell and that the whole world was sacred.

Therefore the duality between what is sacred and not sacred only exists in the mind that sees everything through a dualistic lens in which all things are diametrically opposed to each other.

The true buddha field is not bound to a particular time or location but is the whole universe seen through the lens of the enlightened mind. In that sense, the true buddha field does not exist as the opposite of the ordinary world. Such a buddha field is illusory. Therefore all notions of samsara, nirvana, buddha field, and so on should be investigated by inquiring where they come from, where they are located, and where they go. That inquiry will lead to the realization of the empty nature of all of them, in which they are all illusory, and they have no ground, no root. Then miraculously, one sees the true buddha field, and one will be born in the realm of the true buddha field in that single moment without going anywhere.

The great emptiness, space, is the ground of
samsaric appearances.
All things are as objectless as the sphere of space;
Determine that space is the ground of all.
The pure space is buddhahood.
It is the ground dharmakaya, buddha nature;
Therefore, realize all phenomena are empty.
The sharp vajra of awareness, no-self—
Actualizing that is the full maturity of
ground-residing awareness.

All of samsara is intrinsically empty of svabhava, or intrinsic nature. It lies only in the realm of the mind that is veiled by original ignorance, or not seeing the true nature of reality. In that sense, with this realization, samsara is already collapsing. The truth is that, from the very beginning, the illusion of samsara has no solid ground. That groundlessness is dharmadhatu, or the absolute space from which everything originates and into which everything dissolves. This is none other than the great emptiness, which is the central thought of all Mahayana traditions. Dharmadhatu is described as the primordial state of everything as well as the true nature of reality that is free from the trap of time and place. It goes beyond all conceivable notions such as birth, death, meeting, separation, good, and bad. It cannot be captured by any concept.

There are two versions of reality: conditioned and unconditioned. Everything that our ordinary mind perceives belongs to the conditioned reality. It is constructed with concepts, words, and ideas. Samsara is part of that. Even the very idea of vice and virtue is part of it. True virtue is not even virtue; it goes beyond our idea of virtue. Therefore the whole idea of rejecting vice and cultivating virtue is part of the conditioned.

But this does not literally mean that we should not practice virtue. That could be a dangerous misunderstanding. We should practice virtue as part of the Dharma, the journey to awakening. But cultivating virtue is part of the conditioned and at some point, we have to go beyond everything. That is the radical realization of the unconditioned, the mind beyond the truth, the "concept-crashing truth," the ego-shattering truth. This is why Buddha Samantabhadra became enlightened not by any kind of virtue but simply by awakening to the nature of dharmadhatu, the unconditioned.

Dzogchen and Mahamudra masters remind us that we should not lose touch with the unconditioned on our path, since there is a danger of losing touch with such reality while we are practicing Dharma, cultivating virtue, and so forth. For example, in one of his songs, Milarepa said,

While meditating on Mahamudra,
Do not exert [yourself] in physical and verbal virtuous activities.
There is a danger of losing nonconceptual wisdom.
Rest in the uncontrived, original state.

There is a story about this verse and Milarepa's Dharma regent, Gampopa, who was a doctor and very well-learned even before meeting Milarepa. Gampopa was a monk, and his training was influenced by the Kadampa tradition. Eventually, he journeyed to study with Milarepa, whose style was a radical Mahamudra that did not emphasize outer Dharma practice but more inner Dharma practice—meditation on the nature of mind. He did not encourage his students to perform outward physical religious observations. Gampopa learned this form of Mahamudra from Milarepa.

Then after leaving his guru, Gampopa was hanging around with many pure Kadampa friends, who were very busy with outward religious observances. He felt he had no choice except to go along with them, and he lost all the meditative experiences he had in the past. He started practicing austerities, became very skinny, and lost his immersion in awareness. Then he remembered this verse, and he prayed to his guru Milarepa, reconnecting him with his guru's teachings. From there on, Gampopa was able to come back to his practice and focus more on the radical nondual Mahamudra.

In this verse, Milarepa is not literally encouraging us not to do practices such as generosity or recitation of sutras. He is saying that while doing all these Dharma activities, don't forget to be in touch with the unconditioned. Otherwise, spiritual practices, no matter how beautiful they might be, will not lead us to the ultimate awakening. Similar words were uttered by Longchenpa. He often said one could be bound by both the iron chain of samsara and a golden chain, which refers to our attachment to virtue.

Once one's mind is fully enlightened, the groundless ground is the highest truth, whatever name one might like to give it. It is also the dharmakaya, the highest level of buddhahood, which is free from all forms, all characteristics, and is ineffable. It is sacred but goes beyond all notions of sacred. This verse says that when that understanding is fully matured, that is the highest wisdom that exists, beyond any ordinary wisdom that we can conjure up in our mind.

Afterwards, in order to collapse the structure of grasping and clinging to hope and fear,
Visualize one's three gates as three vajras.
With the essential points, pith instructions, of the three great bindings,
Travel aimlessly through the haunted ground and
Engage in the supreme generosity of offering this cherished body.
This will collapse the false structure of hope and fear.

After such realization is matured, then in order to further enhance such realization as well as to integrate it into one's life, one should engage with the radical practices of Chöd, which intentionally create situations that evoke desires and fears in order to bring our inner demons to light. Sometimes one goes to places that are out of one's comfort zone, where one's worst inner demons, such as fear and attachment, can rise to the surface. Chöd involves taking a journey into places called "haunted grounds," such as cemeteries or the wilderness, in order to practice what is called *lu-jin* (W. *lus sbyin*), a meditative feast of giving one's body away.

What is Chöd? This would be a good time to elucidate the principle of Chöd, which is probably one of the most important parts of Dudjom Lingpa's tradition. He revealed an entire cycle of revelatory teachings and practices of Chöd based on the deity Krodhakali, which are the most widely practiced among all his revelatory writings.

In general, Chöd is considered very radical and transformative, partly because the entire practice is not just theoretical. It invites you to see all of your own inner demons directly on the spot, and at the same time, provides the inner space where you can cut through all of them. As we said, the practice creates situations where you have to face your inner demons, the four maras, and see them clearly. This allows you to be free from the prison of the four maras. *Chöd* means cutting through, but what you cut through is the identification with the inner poisons more than anything. Jamgon Mipham compares this identification to a net that binds us to the four maras the way a fish is caught by a hook. The four maras are the maras of the tangible (or forms), the intangible, elation, and self-conceit.

The first mara is our attachment to the physical world—houses, food, material acquisitions, and electronic gadgets, as well as people; that is, anything we are attached to or have an aversion to, including sense objects that we are either enticed or repulsed by. If you grasp at something, that is attachment, and if you are repulsed by some things, this is also attachment because it means you believe there is an intrinsic truth to them, whereas they are all projections of your own mind.

The mara of the intangible is the attachment to our mental constructs like thoughts, emotions, fantasies. We know they can bind us just like the physical reality can bind us if we don't have the realization of emptiness.

The mara of elation is that joy we experience from fooling ourselves; for example, the joy from believing you are great, or being enchanted by your own achievement, or the rapture or bliss that arises from some spiritual practices or zealous convictions.

The fourth mara is self-conceit, which is totally believing in the existence of the personal self. This version of the four maras is mainly spoken about in Machig Labdron's writings. She said:

Cut through entanglement of objects, the tangible.
Cut through entanglement of mind, the intangible.
Cut through entanglement of grasping, elation.
Cut through entanglement of ego, self-conceit.

Chöd is the most powerful practice to bring about enlightenment or any transformation of consciousness in a short period of time. So much so that Jamgon Mipham praised it by saying that Machig Labdron's path will allow one to actualize, overnight, the fruition that takes a hundred eons by other paths.

Machig Labdron's Chöd is a beautiful integration of the wisdom of the *Prajnaparamita Sutras* and the method of Vajrayana. In the Nyingma tradition, Chöd is also the integration of the wisdom of *Prajnaparamita Sutras*, Dzogchen, and the transformative method of Vajrayana. The practice can allow one to experience extraordinary relief inside as the chain of all hopes and fears is finally broken. Traditionally, Chöd is done with proper instructions from an authentic Chöd master. Then one goes through a process that has beginning, middle, and ending stages in order to complete the journey.

The practice begins with establishing a sacred, nondual view toward one's body, speech, and mind. *Vajra* in this verse means sacred. This corresponds to the fundamental philosophy of Vajrayana, which is to regard all things as sacred. By entering into this view, one is naturally deconstructing one's ego identity as a separate self in order to merge with egoless, nondual awareness, where one is in touch with the unconditioned state of one's being, which has never been bound by kleshas. With that awareness, we can then engage with Chöd practices such as traveling into haunted grounds or places that scare us.

Three Suppressions

This practice is also known as the three suppressions, (the "three great bindings"), which are the initial suppression, the middle suppression, and the final suppression. First you enter into a state of pure awareness with visualizations, such as visualizing yourself as Vajrayogini or Krodhakali and other visualizations. Then you imagine consecrating the ground as a perfect place for the journey and bring all the demons and gods, which are the archetypical representations of everyone's neuroses, under your power. In other words, you suppress them. In this context, the traditional Chöd texts describe suppression as having three aspects: bringing the place, the archetypes of demons, and the self under the power of your own awareness.

The three suppressions are to be done gradually and successively. The sacred suppression is done from the beginning of entering the haunted ground and covers the whole journey, including when you move to another haunted ground. In other words, the three suppressions cover the entire journey from beginning to end in the haunted ground. The three suppressions involve very precise visualizations that are not covered in this book. One would need to read a Chöd text for more details.

Ground Dharmakaya

All the inquiries as well as the radical practice of Chöd have one single goal in the end: to lead us to the actualization of ground dharmakaya. The term *actualization* in Tibetan has a very specific meaning. It indicates that one is no longer conceptualizing a teaching but is embodying it. This chapter is about not just philosophizing or meditating on ground dharmakaya but truly embodying it and becoming it.

Ground dharmakaya is a term used quite extensively in Dzogchen writings. *Ground* refers to something that is already there originally. From that point of view, ground dharmakaya is another name for buddha nature. In the end, it is always important to bear in mind that the path of Dzogchen is leading us to realize buddha nature—which is none other than the pure luminous nature of our mind—if not right now, then in this very lifetime. It is the target of this path of Dzogchen. Remember not to miss it, and keep giving your attention to it.

From the *Sharp Vajra of Awareness Tantra*, the third chapter on the actualization of the ground dharmakaya.

IV. The Characteristic and Quality of Ground

The nature of all apparent existence is emptiness.
The great emptiness is naturally complete within
the nature of the path.

The previous chapter asserts that all existence is naturally empty of svabhava. Such emptiness is the true nature of everything that our mind can possibly imagine, from the most ordinary to the most extraordinary. It is the absolute truth that is always present without any limitations of time. Therefore there is no need to arrive at a particular destination to discover it. If only our mind can see it, it is here right now. Realizing this is the final goal of the spiritual journey as well as the path itself. It is both the path and the destination. This is why the realization of emptiness is regarded as the supreme path.

Emptiness spoken of here is more than just negation or deconstruction of svabhava. It is also the great emptiness that transcends all mental proliferation and every concept. In the end, it is not even negation. In the beginning, when we meditate on emptiness, it is usually about negating something such as the self or svabhava. But the absolute truth is more than negation. It goes beyond any kind of comprehension, beyond either negation or affirmation. In Buddhist logic, there are two mental functions that we often use to understand something. They are called affirmation, "it is…" and negation, "it is not…" Yet both are still workings of our thinking mind. To truly experience emptiness, we need to go beyond this mind's function completely.

Therefore the great emptiness is completely beyond the reach of our thinking mind. It is not just nothing, not just the absence of svabhava but also the unity of everything—ordinary and extraordinary, relative and absolute, form and emptiness, nirvana and samsara, buddhas and sentient beings. This is also the true dharmakaya, or buddha nature, or *tathagatagarba*.

The essence, dharmakaya-buddha nature,
Is beyond being altered or contrived by either samsara or nirvana,
Free from all conceptual extremes, endowed with the three gates of liberation.
The five kayas, five families, five wisdoms,
Five buddha fields, five fathers, five mothers, three jewels,
The three roots, enlightened families, mandalas, empowerment, propitiation—
They are all naturally complete within the nature of Maha Yoga.

In Dzogchen, there is the nature of our mind that is the dharmakaya-buddha nature. It is always present, and nothing can condition it. It has many names. Sometimes it is called self-arisen awareness. Dharmakaya-buddha nature is the nature of all things and is unconditioned; there are no events or circumstances that can alter its true nature. Not even kleshas and the sufferings of the world can contaminate it or make it less than what it is. Nor can the virtues of the Buddha make it more sublime than it is.

Therefore, on the spiritual journey, while cultivating good deeds, our consciousness is undoubtedly transforming but the dharmakaya that resides in each of us is the same. It's not that our virtue is making it more sublime or exalted.

On the other hand, even in those moments of getting lost in our kleshas, becoming confused or miserable, our condition is not making the tathagatagarba or buddha nature in us less sublime. In that sense, it is our true nature, always complete and perfect in itself, regardless of what is happening in our lives. It does not really change.

This can sometimes be very difficult to understand. As human beings, we are so identified with the conditions of our being, which are contingent on outer and inner factors. As far as we know, who we are is related to our ordinary experiences of ourselves—the state of our body, our moods, our circumstances, or if we've done some psychoanalysis, maybe our shadow. We identify with all of these. Our everyday mind does not capture a whole other dimension of our being, which turns out to be who we really are. It's not the mind, it's not the body, it's not the thoughts, it's not our karma. Yet we cannot say it is separate from any of them. Separation is duality. The idea of something to be separated from is already dualistic.

There is also, of course, our relative self that is based on the building blocks of our body, size, shape, age, birth, death, and personal history. They are all true to a certain extent. We all have parents and some place where we were born. Someone writes down our birthdate. Someone will even remember our death date, even if we won't remember it. But our true nature, the dharmakaya within, transcends all these seemingly solid, earthly realities. Our true nature has no birthdate and never dies, even though it is not some kind of entity. It is called *unborn*. The unborn only can be discovered when all notions of self are dissolved, including the doctrinaire self, such as the higher self, or soul.

The unborn is the unconditioned, or ultimate truth, which is the quintessential view of all Mahayana teachings. This is also true for Dudjom Lingpa's tradition. One time, Tulku Drimed Ozer, the son and Dharma regent of Dudjom Lingpa, met with Lerab Lingpa, who was also a scholar. They had a philosophical dialogue that lasted for a few days. At one point Lerab Lingpa said, "Some of your students are disgracing your father, their guru, by preaching an inauthentic doctrine. Since you are his son, I will have a dialogue with you to understand whether you understand your father's view or not. Tell me now—how do you define view, meditation, conduct, and fruition?"

Tulku Drimed Ozer replied, "View is to determine that everything is the unborn. Meditation is to maintain a state that goes beyond even the concept of distraction. Conduct is to train in the way of the unceasing. Fruition is to be established in that which is beyond mind."

Then Lerab Lingpa was extremely happy and said, "This is what the saying 'the son follows in the footsteps of the father' should be like."

Usually an entire doctrine can be completely described in the system of the four: view, meditation, conduct, and fruition. It was amazing that Tulku Drimed Ozer was able to recite the system of his father's tradition spontaneously in an eloquent and pithy way. No wonder Lerab Lingpa was impressed.

The unborn is a synonym for the ultimate truth or emptiness across Mahayana traditions. It describes the ultimate truth beyond any conditions, such as birth. This is also true in Dzogchen, where the term *unborn* is used quite widely as a synonym for dharmakaya-buddha nature.

Dharmakaya-buddha nature is the great emptiness that, because it is ineffable, is also free from the eight conceptual extremes, known in Tibetan as *trö pé ta gyé* (W. *spros pa'i mtha' brgyad*). They are: arising and ceasing, nonexistence and permanence, coming and going, being multiple and being single.

This great emptiness also has three attributes, known as the three gates of liberation, or *namthar go sum* (W. *rnam thar sgo gsum*). The three gates are emptiness, absence of characteristics, and absence of expectations. An earlier chapter described the three gates, and there are also other books that describe them in more detail. The three gates of liberation have a variety of interpretations but in essence, they are negating svabhava in all things. The purpose of understanding the three gates is to bring about an inner freedom that goes beyond both hope and fear, because hope and fear are basically a product of holding onto the notion that there is something real to be desired or afraid of.

The idea that the great emptiness is free from the eight extremes of conceptual proliferation and endowed with the three gates of liberation is pointing out what emptiness *is not*. Yet that emptiness is fully rich and is the embodiment of the five kayas, the five buddha families, and the five wisdoms. These describe what the great emptiness *is*.

Maha Yoga

This verse is saying that all these enlightened principles are already complete within Maha Yoga, which is one of the six tantric classes in the Nyingma tradition. In the Nyingma tradition, there are nine yanas, or vehicles, that take us to nirvana. They are also paths that come with systems of doctrines and observations. In the nine-yana system, the last three, Maha Yoga, Anu Yoga, and Ati Yoga, are called the three inner classifications, *nang gyü dé sum* (W. *nang rgyud sde gsum*). Not only are they tantric systems, but they are the more advanced tantric systems. These three yanas are also considered part of Anuttarayoga Tantra, the Unsurpassable Tantra, which is extremely rich and involves a variety of transformative techniques. Some are elaborate and some are utterly simple.

What is Maha Yoga? Its doctrine is a nondual, sacred outlook that asserts that not only is everything empty of svabhava, but the whole world and existence are naturally sacred. Its practice emphasizes the generation, or creation, stage of Vajrayana, *utpatti-krama*, which is the first of the two stages in Anuttarayoga Tantra.

The creation stage is sometimes called *contrived yoga* because it is a meditative system through which we manufacture sacred imagery in our mind, such as forms of deities and mandalas, in order to purify our perception of the ordinariness of all things.

As a habit of dualism, our ordinary mind tends to see a fundamental duality between sacred and mundane. It often sees the existing world, including our body, as quite ordinary. Sometimes even religious traditions developed doctrines that view everything in this world as impure or flawed. One of the objectives of creation-stage yoga is to uproot this dualistic perception, which is a partial as well as even an erroneous view of the world. Dualism is a very powerful habit that is rooted in our minds and requires powerful methods, such as utpatti-krama, to uproot it. But this method is contrived, since the deities we visualize are not real either; they are manufactured in our mind. So eventually we need to go beyond it. It is not the ultimate path as it still relies on methods that are contrived.

This whole concept might be hard to understand unless you are a well-seasoned Vajrayana practitioner, but there is an anecdote that may help you understand how the method works. Once someone came to me during a meditation retreat in Santa Cruz, a beautiful beach town in Northern California. She said that she was having issues with her landlord. Every time she had an interaction with him, she felt very uneasy, and this was problematic for her. There were not any unpleasant situations that happened, but she just felt uneasy. I sat for a while and prayed that the right answer would come through. I felt that there was no real danger to her from her landlord, based on her sharing. She only had a feeling of unease around him. I suggested to her, "Next time you encounter him, just visualize Avalokiteshvara, the Buddha of love." After several months, she came back to me and said, "It worked."

This worked because most likely she had some projections about her landlord that had nothing to do with the reality of what was happening. Perhaps in his presence something was triggered inside of her. Somehow, the visualization was able to change her perception of her landlord that had been colored by her own mind. Once the problem was gone, she didn't have to continuously visualize her landlord as Avalokiteshvara every time she ran into him. It was an expedient method.

In the bigger picture, we all tend to perceive the whole world through a dualistic perception that sees the world as divided into sacred and secular. This is not just how we see the outside world but also ourselves. So utpatti-krama can help us to let go of such perceptions by viewing the whole world through the eye of the sacred and seeing it as the mandala, and ourselves and all sentient beings as deities.

Sacred Principles

Utpatti-krama is built upon a rich system of sacred principles, such as five families, three or five kayas, and so forth. The five-fold sacred principles—five families, five wisdoms, five buddha fields, five father buddhas, five mother buddhas—are different aspects of buddha nature, or great emptiness, that can be actualized in our own experience. Many of the Vajrayana techniques are built upon the idea of all-pervasive sacredness and offer methods to allow the practitioner to truly embody buddha nature with all the enlightened principles. These systems are the essential building blocks of Maha Yoga.

For example, as one continues to practice Vajrayana, one would be working with techniques where all these sacred categories like the five families or five wisdoms would be incorporated. There might be times where you visualize the five families in conjunction with the five wisdoms. This is just one example; in Maha Yoga there are other deities and mandalas that one would visualize as symbolic expressions of wisdom in order to let go of our impure perception of the world.

Remember as you read this text that the main theme of the *Sharp Vajra Tantra* is primarily an illumination of Dzogchen. Yet it describes all the different yanas and techniques as different ways that could lead to the moment when we are ready to practice and realize the wisdom of Dzogchen. Dzogchen in this context is the main objective, the main destination, and all other techniques described here are part of Dzogchen because they can be regarded as different ways to get to the point where we are ready to practice Dzogchen.

Also, this text is pointing out that the wisdom of Dzogchen contains everything; nothing is missing in it. Indeed, the essential principles of all the yanas are already complete in Dzogchen as the all-encompassing vehicle, and this is why it is called the Great Completion. While there are other ways of defining Dzogchen, this is the way that Dudjom Lingpa defines it. In this definition, all the other yanas are partial compared to Dzogchen. They do not capture the profundity of Dzogchen. This is described by an analogy, used by many Dzogchen masters, of someone sitting on the top of the king of all mountains. From that spot, you see the tops of all the mountains around you. But if you sit on the smaller mountains around the king of mountains, you will not see the top of that great mountain.

Let's look at the different sacred categories that are mentioned in this verse.

Five Kayas

The five kayas, or *panchakaya,* are dharmakaya, sambhogakaya, nirmanakaya, *avikara-vajrakaya* (immutable vajra body), and *abhisambodhikaya* (fully enlightened body). *Kaya* means body but in this context, it refers to a state or dimension of enlightenment. Three of the kayas are widely known across all Mahayana traditions: dharmakaya, sambhogakaya, and nirmanakaya. While there are countless definitions of either the three or five kayas in numerous texts, their essence is the same. In the end, the five kayas describe the nature of enlightenment that is freed from all obscurations and endowed with qualities such as love and wisdom.

Five Buddha Families

The five families are based on the mandala of the buddhas, yet they are also just different aspects of enlightened mind or buddha mind, which are being expressed in sacred configurations or forms. The five families are known as the Buddha, Vajra, Ratna, Padma, and Karma families. In Vajrayana, there are often specific mandalas or deities associated with each of the families. Even though they are called families, such a category is not describing separate enlightened minds. They are simply describing various nuances of buddha mind.

The Buddha family represents the dimension of buddha mind that is free from all duality and from any limitation that our mind can imagine—birth, death, meeting, separation, good and bad, and so forth.

The Vajra family is the very nature of buddha mind that is unlike any conditioned phenomena. In that sense, it is beyond change because it is not a conditioned phenomenon in the first place.

Buddha mind is not merely free from all limitations; it is enriched with enlightened qualities. That factor is represented by the Ratna family. *Ratna* literally means jewel, which is often a symbol of desirable qualities and abundance.

Buddha mind is also free from all the inner obscurations and kleshas, symbolized by the Padma, or Lotus, family. The lotus is often used as a symbol for purity because even though it grows in the mud, it is not contaminated by the mud and blossoms beautifully.

Buddha mind is also the source from which all enlightened activities emerge, even though it is free from any egoic intention to act. The motive behind enlightened activities is no longer the ego but rather enlightened mind itself. This is the Karma family.

The explanation above is a more standard explanation that is in alignment with many Vajrayana systems. These five buddha families can also be explained from the Dzogchen point of view, which is much more experiential. Dzogchen points out that these five buddha families are within our own consciousness right now. For example, in Dzogchen they invite us to recognize the unhindered, spacious, empty, ceaseless state of present awareness as each of the buddha families. This makes them much more experiential and not so theoretical.

Five Wisdoms

The five wisdoms are not mutually exclusive from each other but are different attributes of enlightened mind. The five wisdoms are the wisdom of dharmadhatu, mirror-like wisdom, wisdom of equality, wisdom of discernment, and wisdom of accomplishment.

Generally speaking, these five wisdoms describe buddha mind by including its nature as well as all its nuances and attributes. The definition of each of the wisdoms is very influenced by the system or tradition that one is using as a philosophical base. So it is important not to hold on to one definition. Various masters and texts give unique definitions of the five wisdoms.

Here, one could say that the wisdom of dharmadhatu is the very nature of mind, which is already pure and free from all obscurations. It doesn't need to be changed, fixed, or improved in any way. Mirror-like wisdom means that buddha mind is not like a dead or abstract entity but rather, it has the ability to reflect and be aware of everything. Just like images shine in a mirror, everything can be seen in the boundless field of buddha mind.

The wisdom of equality means that while buddha mind sees all things, it doesn't categorize or judge anything that it sees. Instead, it sees all things through the eye of equality. It sees both samsara and nirvana, yet it sees they are the same in their true nature. In other words, the wisdom of equality is the nondual lens of buddha mind that sees the whole reality, whereas unenlightened mind sees everything through the lens of duality.

The wisdom of discernment means that buddha mind is not a mindless mind that sees everything merged and mingled together as if the whole universe is like mashed potatoes. Buddha mind is not a mindless state but has amazing intelligence that can discern everything. For example, if you are in the state of enlightened mind, you might look at the computer screen and see the computer while seeing that its nature is empty of any true existence. But you can see that it is a computer and that it is not a wall. So buddha mind doesn't say, "It's all the same, so I can look at either the computer screen or the wall," when one is on a computer video call. That doesn't work. The wisdom of discernment sees everything as the same empty essence but sees the nuances, the complex nature of all that exists.

The wisdom of accomplishment means that buddha mind is not an inactive or passive state of mind that simply indulges in some cozy eternal peace. Instead, it is filled with motive, power, strength, and insight to engage with actions that will benefit everyone. This is more than just a profound insight. Enlightened mind is filled with the impulse of compassion that motivates one to help others.

Five Buddha Fields

The five buddha fields are not mundane, physical realms. In Tantric Buddhist language, they are *mandalas,* or enlightened realms of the buddhas. They are purely a state of the awakened mind. There is often a relationship between the five buddha families and the five buddha fields. The five buddha fields are Akanishtha, Abhirati, Shrimati, Sukhavati, and Karmaprasiddhi. They are the enlightened mind being described in the form of sacred realms where nothing is ordinary, and everyone is a buddha or bodhisattva. Even rocks and mountains are no longer ordinary but are sacred. The minds of every resident in those realms are utterly full of love and wisdom.

Remember, this is the experience of the enlightened mind, and that's why it is described as this perfect, problem-free, idyllic world. For example, a verse from the *Guhyagarbha Tantra* captures this principle. It says,

Without a self-arisen awareness knowing the true reality,
even the realms of the Sugatas appear as lower realms.
At the moment the meaning of dharmata-equality
is realized,
even the lower realms are joyous Akanishtha.

This verse basically explains the whole idea of buddha fields in the most pithy way. Without such understanding, we could end up with all kinds of erroneous notions about buddha fields. The verse reminds us that the true buddha fields are not physical worlds but are the utterly enlightened mind that sees the empty yet sacred nature of all things.

The truth is that this state of consciousness resides in each of us. If we know how to abide in that state regardless of what is happening, we can be completely calm, and we won't be lost in fear or confusion. Many of you perhaps have experienced this. But even if you don't have that experience, it is powerful to trust that there is a state of consciousness in each of us that is completely free, liberated. It is an extraordinary place. So at least we can just trust that it is there.

Many Buddhist liturgies describe buddha fields. They can seem like particular physical locations, but their underlying meaning is the perfect sacred realm within where there is no fear, there is no suffering, and where everything is sacred. While that place resides in each of us, sometimes we have to imagine it in a particular form in order to move our attention toward it. Visualizing these buddha fields helps us develop an affinity with it, and to have the aspiration to be in such an enlightened state of mind where we are no longer challenged, we are no longer reacting, and we are no longer gripped by our thoughts and emotions.

Five Father Buddhas

The five father buddhas in Vajrayana are also representations of different qualities of enlightened mind. Their principles are similar to the five wisdoms and five buddha families. But they are used as objects of samadhi or meditation in Vajrayana sadhanas as well as a doorway to the awakening to all-pervasive sacredness, the fulcrum of Vajrayana.

All-pervasive sacredness is the view that everything is sacred, from the most beautiful to the most repulsive objects perceived by our ordinary mind. Here the principle of the five father buddhas is applied as a model or system to bring about awakening to the sacredness of the five skandhas, or five aggregates, the very things that our being consists of—form, feeling, perception, mental formation, and consciousness. In our ordinary life, we do not see any sacredness in them, and in some religious doctrines, the five skandhas are regarded as mundane and intrinsically flawed. Even some Buddhist sutras don't say anything about the sacredness of the five skandhas.

Take feeling, or *vedana*, as an example. Some texts say feeling is intrinsically samsaric and assert that feelings are naturally sorrowful, even pleasant ones, because they are caused by karma and kleshas. They are part of samsara, or the vicious circle of suffering. Whereas in Vajrayana, feeling is regarded as intrinsically sacred, and we are also sacred. Everything about us is sacred—our mind, our body, our senses, our world, our environment. Therefore, the five father buddhas correspond to the sacredness of each skandha by asserting, for example, that form is Vajrasattva, feeling is Ratnasambhava, perception is Amitabha, mental formation is Amoghasiddhi, and consciousness is Vairochana. This is the true way of understanding the principle of the five father buddhas. Moving away from this understanding would only lead us far from the true meaning of who they are.

Sometimes people could have a theistic attitude toward the five buddhas, believing they are actual sublime beings who reside in some celestial dimension. One might even know intellectually that they are not supernatural beings, yet the possibility of an unconscious theistic understanding could be lurking in the dark recesses of one's mind. Such misconstrued understanding becomes a beautiful and powerful obstacle to true awakening. Those who practice Vajrayana must let go of every speck of theistic tendency in order to develop an authentic nondual attitude to the tantric deities.

The whole method of liberation in Vajrayana is to cut through our attachment to anything; that is, to cut through our deep habit of reifying. If we reify not just the illusions in our life but even the tantric deities, it would be an obstacle to full awakening. Yet it is easy to get lost in the path of reifying because it speaks to our primitive human impulses and gives a tremendous sense of mental comfort, which is hard for our ego to resist.

If those deities are not supernatural beings, what are their forms about? In Vajrayana, their forms are not considered the true deity but are considered the symbolic deity, *tsen ma tak kyi lha* (W. *mtshan ma rtags kyi lha*). The true deity of nature of reality lies within. The pure, luminous nature of our mind is considered to be the true deity, *chö nyi dön gyi lha* (W. *chos nyid don gyi lha*).

Instructions for Meditating on Deities

Then one may wonder what is the use of having the forms in the first place if the true deity has no form? The forms are a means to invoke awakening to the pure, luminous nature of our mind as well as wholesome states of mind. In Vajrayana, when one meditates on the deities, one should actually train one's mind to remember the connection between the symbolic forms of the deities and the significance that lies behind them.

Imagine that you are meditating on Avalokiteshvara. First, you learn to visualize Avalokiteshvara clearly as described in the sadhana. Not only that, the instruction is to visualize the form as if it is made out of rainbow light, which helps you to not solidify the deity.

Second, you remember that each detail of Avalokiteshvara's form has significance. For example, the four arms symbolize the four immeasurables: immeasurable love, immeasurable compassion, immeasurable empathetic joy, and immeasurable equanimity.

The third step is that you remember that Avalokiteshvara is inside and that your true nature is Avalokiteshvara. That awareness is called vajra pride. This is not ordinary pride based on ego. It is called vajra pride because there is unshakable confidence that you are the true Avalokiteshvara, which is bodhicitta, the awakened heart. This becomes the catalyst for invoking bodhicitta within.

Unless someone already has a strong affinity for these deities in Vajrayana, they may not be able to immediately understand the transformative power of meditation on those deities. Therefore, to truly benefit from such a practice, you need to go through the process of training the mind with these three instructions: visualize the deity clearly, remember the significance of the details, and remember the deity is your true nature. Then there is a point when the sacred forms begin to work powerfully in your consciousness, and you have immediate access to the qualities that these deities represent.

Five Mother Buddhas

The five mother buddhas also represent all-pervasive sacredness. This sacred outlook is, of course, held in Vajrayana in general, but it is emphasized in the Nyingma Tantras, which often calls this *nang si dak nyam chen pö tawa* (W. *snang srid dag mnyam chen po'i lta ba*), the view of the great sacredness and equality of all apparent existence. This is well-taught in the *Guhyagarbha Tantra,* which establishes the relationship between the five mother buddhas and the five elements in the context of all-pervasive sacredness. It asserts that earth is Buddhalochana, water is Mamaki, fire is Pandaravasini, wind is Samayatara, and space is Dhatvishvari. In this way, the five buddha mothers illuminate the sacred and pure nature of everything that exists around us.

It seems that the world has two sides even though it is, in essence, one. One side is what is perceived by enlightened mind and the other side is what is perceived by unenlightened mind. Sacredness is not seen by unenlightened mind, so you might say, "Sacredness lies in the eyes of the beholder," as it is only seen by the eyes of the enlightened mind. In our ordinary mind, there is often a duality between sacred and secular, or ordinary, things. But this division does not really lie in the realm of reality. It is again superimposed by our own mind. We often project sacredness onto something else, feeling that we are not part of it, or we are devoid of it. The principle of the five mother buddhas is that the sacred pervades everything that exists.

Three Jewels

The three jewels are, in general Buddhist doctrine, the Buddha, Dharma, and Sangha. Buddha here doesn't have to be singular; it can be plural—buddhas. Buddha doesn't have to be limited to one master or deity. In the mind of most people, Buddha refers to someone who is fully enlightened. But in the deeper meaning, Buddha actually refers to the dharmakaya, the unborn Buddha, which is the pure, luminous nature of mind.

Generally speaking, Dharma is the path to the awakening, but Dharma is not, in that sense, any kind of religious system. It is our own inner journey in which we purify our consciousness to develop wisdom and compassion. The idea of Dharma can sometimes be very subtle and profound, and it can easily elude our ability to understand it.

Sangha is often understood as the spiritual fellowship on our journey. In today's world, people regard their spiritual community as their sangha, and people who live in a monastery regard everyone in their monastery as part of their sangha. But in the Mahayana system, Sangha refers to the fellowship of awakened bodhisattvas. There is undeniable benefit in taking refuge in outside conducive conditions for our inner awakening not as the ultimate refuge but rather as a temporary refuge. We can take refuge in the Sangha as traveling companions on our journey but not as the ultimate refuge.

In Dzogchen, Buddha, Dharma, and Sangha are no longer seen as something outside of yourself. They are already complete in the pure nature of your mind. In that sense, there is no separation between the three jewels. The pure, luminous nature of your mind is the Buddha, Dharma, and Sangha. It is the embodiment of the three jewels. This understanding is the true way of taking refuge. Otherwise, you will be a refugee eternally, which you don't want to be! When you take refuge with this true understanding, you will not be a refugee, you will be a Dharmakaya Buddha. How can the Dharmakaya Buddha be a refugee?

Three Roots

The three roots are unique to Vajrayana. They are the guru, deva, and dakini. The guru often refers to the master who bestows the tantric initiation known as *abhisheka*. *Deva*, or chosen deity, refers to a tantric deity such as Vajrakilaya. *Dakini*, or sky-dancer, is also a deity that is mentioned in tantric literature. Vajrayana often says that the guru is the source of blessing, the deva is the source of siddhis, and the dakini is the one who removes obstacles on the path. But again, in the true sense, these three roots are already within each of us. Again, one can say that the luminous pure nature of mind is the true guru, the true deva, and the true dakini.

The term *guru* has many meanings. Sometimes, as we said, it refers to a human guru from whom you received abhisheka, or initiation; in Dzogchen, it might be the one who gave you pointing-out instructions. Sometimes *guru* refers to your lineage gurus. There is also a notion of the *rang rig dön gyi lama* (W. *rang rig don gyi bla ma*), the self-knowing awareness, the ultimate guru. This term is extensively used in Dzogchen teachings, which is indicating that the ultimate guru does not reside outside yourself, but that your own pure awareness is the ultimate guru.

There are also devotional practices in Vajrayana called guru yoga. While devotion is generated in relationship to one's guru, the outside guru is merely a bridge between you and your inner guru, the Dharmakaya Buddha, your true nature.

In the body, with the five arrangements,
The purification and transmutation of the nadi, prana,
and bindu;
The path of blazing and dripping;
Empowerments; and the four [kinds of] bliss
Are all spontaneously present as the
play of buddha nature.

This verse offers a synthesis of Anu Yoga, the second of the three inner tantras, which mainly emphasizes the completion stage of

Vajrayana, or *sampanna-krama.* This is a system that utilizes one's physical and psychic, or subtle, body as a means of purification.

Tantric systems teach that the body has a subtle dimension of *nadi*, *prana*, and *bindu*, [in Tibetan, *tsa*, *lung*, and *tiglé* (W. *rtsa*, *rlung*, and *thig le*)], or channels, energies, and essences. Each of these—nadi, prana, and bindu—have functions for maintaining our life. They are the subtle building blocks of our being and with the right methods, they can be utilized as powerful vessels for inner purification and awakening rather than as the basis of samsara.

There are numerous nadis, or channels; some tantric systems say there are a hundred thousand of them. Channels have different functions; one of them is to enable the prana to move through our system.

The prana, also called energy, or wind, is the vital energy force in our system, and it too has a variety of functions. Basically it enables us to live and engage with life's activities. It is the very force that allows our consciousness to interact with objects such as forms, sounds, and so forth. Therefore, it is known as the vehicle for our consciousness. Even our physical movement is possible because of prana.

The ultimate bindu is the dharmadhatu, free from all limitations, the state of nonduality, which is not material or physical. It is not even a thing. However, bindu is also described as a subtle element that resides in our channels and can be the cause of a variety of experiences. Bindu also can be a factor for inner awakening when the right method is applied. This is why in Vajrayana, one takes refuge not only in the usual enlightened principles, such as the three jewels and three kayas, but also in the nadi, prana, and bindu.

Sometimes people find this perplexing—how can you take refuge in your subtle body? It is because Vajrayana uses the subtle body as a shortcut to enlightenment. For example, the Anu Yoga system uses our subtle body as a powerful vessel for radical purification and awakening. It is more powerful than any other medium we could find outside. When someone truly understands the doctrine and application of Anu Yoga, one can experience a powerful awakening, such as undoing the knots of all the channels, and experience bodhicitta, or enlightened mind. This is why we can take refuge in our subtle body—nadi, prana, bindu—as a vessel for enlightenment.

Some might think that we are taking refuge in them because their true nature is sacred. That seems convincing but it is more than that in the context of Anu Yoga. Otherwise, since Vajrayana teaches that everything is sacred, we could be taking refuge in rocks, yak dung, garbage cans, and so forth. But those things won't take us anywhere the way the subtle body can in Anu Yoga.

A Visualization

Brief techniques are mentioned in this chapter, such as visualizing your body as the deity. Within that, you mentally construct the three channels—the central channel and two on either side of it, in Sanskrit, *avadhuti, rasana, lalana,* or in Tibetan, *wuma, roma, kyangma* (W. *dbu ma, ro ma, rkyang ma*).

One method—"blazing and dripping"—is to imagine the five chakras, or wheels of the nadis, which are located vertically in our subtle body. At the bottom of the central channel, visualize a symbol called *ah-shed* (W. *ah shad*), which resembles a narrow triangle wider at one end. Then imagine fire blazes forth from it. Simultaneously, visualize *hang* ཧཾ at the upper end of the central channel.

Then the wisdom wind or prana enters your central channel, enhancing the fire, and reaches the *hang* ཧཾ. Ambrosia, *amrita*, flows down, which is a symbol of enlightened mind, the union of bliss and emptiness. This bliss is not just ordinary bliss; it has different levels and interpretations. This particular bliss is unique to Vajrayana and is not openly talked about in Buddhist sutras, whereas emptiness, of course, is often mentioned in them. The purpose of generating bliss is to purify subtle, internal obscurations and experience a full and matured form of awakening.

This whole method purifies one's nadi, prana, and bindu, transmuting nadi into nirmanakaya, prana into sambhogakaya, and bindu into dharmakaya. Such transmutation is a state in which our samsaric habits stored in our subtle body are dissolved, and our subtle body returns to its natural state, which is already pure, enlightened, and sacred. Vajrayana teaches that the true nature of our mind as well as our subtle body is already pure and enlightened but just like our mind, our subtle body is temporarily bound by samsaric habits. This bondage is not the true nature of our subtle body.

One example that we can use is water, whose nature is pristine and flowing. If it freezes from exposure to cold, then it is contracted and doesn't flow any more. But it remains as water, and when it is melted again with conditions like heat, then water flows. You could say then that water returns to its natural state. In the same way, you can say that this transmutation of nadi, prana, and bindu into nirmanakaya, sambhogakaya, and dharmakaya is returning our subtle body to its natural state, which is already pure.

In essence, dharmakaya is the space,
free from all the signs,
Yet, in accordance with samsara, the bondage of
names and forms [is taught]
In order to lead those who, grasping at permanence,
are to be tamed.

In order to refrain from the six fixations,
The entrance of samsara will be blocked by the three: clarity, purity, and emptiness.

The dharmakaya, or the highest Buddha, not only has no form but is also beyond any kind of conceptual signs. It is the absolute truth endowed with the three gates of liberation, beyond all limitations that our mind can create. Dharmakaya, in that sense, is just the pure dimension of the nature of mind. It doesn't even have the slightest form, color, shape, or mandala. It is not like a physical Buddha that has attributes. But here in Vajrayana, mandalas of deities are depicted in particular forms with bodies, enlightened activities, and retinues. How does that come to be when the true Buddha, the dharmakaya, is void of any of them?

The answer is that such forms are manifested in order to help those who are attached to duality, or who have a tendency to reify reality. It helps those people find a way to the absolute truth because without such forms, they would not be able to have any idea of dharmakaya. So the form becomes a bridge between them and dharmakaya.

Therefore, even dharmakaya is manifested in a form such as a deity that has gender, a palace or kingdom, and a retinue, like a royal family in ancient India. If you were able to journey to ancient India, the royal arrangement might resemble a mandala. In the center would be the sovereign lord of the kingdom, which in the mandala is the main deity. The sovereign lord would be sitting on a throne presiding over the whole assembly and surrounded by ministers, servants, and noble lords. Similarly, in the mandala, the deity is surrounded by a retinue.

In the end, the creation of deity and mandala is not meant to lead people to solidify the forms as a divine reality that replaces ordinary reality. Its purpose is the reverse. Its purpose is to transcend attachment to forms. Here the text is saying that the whole creation is used to cut through the six fixations—the attachment to the six forms of physical reality including form, sound, smell, touch, taste, and phenomena.

This is a bit ironic because on the one hand, it involves the process of creating a non-material reality, a sacred form of deity and mandala, but its purpose is to use that creation to cut through attachment to physical reality that is neither ordinary nor sacred. The question is, why not cut through attachment right there on the spot? Why create a sacred form in order to cut through attachment to form? Because the human mind tends to be very conceptual and dualistic, it often has difficulty understanding anything nonconceptual like dharmakaya. It always works through concepts or what we call signs, where reality is divided, dissected, and given names and characteristics.

The idea of using duality to go beyond duality is spoken about through analogies in the tantras, such as using iron to cut through iron. The second iron represents our dualistic perception of reality that reifies everything. The first iron symbolizes the tantric methods, which come with a lot of complex knowledge and techniques—a sacred duality. The idea is not to reify that sacred duality but use it to completely cut through the dualistic perception of reality. Here it is saying that mandala creation is similar to that. The purpose is not to construct sacred duality but to transcend everything in order to be in touch with the true nature of reality, where all duality is dissolved.

In general, we are trapped in our attachment to the senses and the world perceived through our mind. Our mind constructs a dualistic view of reality, either imagined or felt through our senses, and is very attached to that view. That attachment is the very thing that binds us, and that bondage is very difficult to break.

There are, of course, radical nondual traditions that invite us to engage with effortlessness, no-practice practice, to cut through such attachment. That works for many people, but often it is hard for people to cut through such attachment directly unless they engage with methods that have some commonality with their attachment. Cutting through attachment directly is most shocking to our default tendencies. It's like someone who has been locked up for ages in a dungeon and then is suddenly taken out into the sun. They may not be able to tolerate it. Instead, they may need gradual steps so they feel comfortable enough to come out and see the bright sun.

In the end, the practice of deity yoga will lead to the realization that the true deity is not even a deity and has no characteristics or conceptual signs. It doesn't matter if you construct a deity with a form or not; as long as you give it characteristics, it has conceptual signs. That deity is not the dharmakaya. Yet we can use the conceptual signs to transcend them. This is the purpose of deity yoga.

Three Principles in Creation Stage

The creation of the mandala, which is part of the creation stage, or utpatti-krama, is based on three principles: clarity, purity, and emptiness. Clarity and purity were discussed earlier in the three instructions for meditating on the deities.

Clarity refers to creating the mandala in one's mind as clearly as one can, without missing any attributes of the sacred form, and as vividly as if you are looking directly at the real form. In the old days, people spent a lot of time learning how to create the deity's form in their mind clearly and in as much detail as possible. Often, during the tantric sadhana, in addition to the prayers, there are guided meditations that lead a practitioner to construct the mandala of the deity in his or her mind.

The second principle is remembrance of purity. Not only is the deity clearly visualized in your mind, but you also remember the significance of the colors, the face, the posture, the implements of the deity and so forth. For example, many of the tantric deities have three eyes, which often represent the three kayas. The implements in the hands represent enlightened principles; for example, the butcher's knife, or *kartika,* represents the wisdom that cuts through the very root of samsara.

The last principle is emptiness, which means that the form is devoid of any kind of solidity or substantiality. Even though it is appearing, you remember that it is not concrete. We are not supposed to solidify the images. Therefore often during visualizations in utpatti-krama, the instructions indicate that the deities should be visualized as if they are made of light. They have no solidity but are completely translucent without one speck made of atoms.

The three principles are a radical method to actualize what is called "blocking the entrance to samsara." This is a term that occurs quite often in Nyingma sadhanas and writings. It has the connotation of using a radical method that immediately stops one's consciousness from descending into a samsaric state of mind.

Therefore, all the contrived, provisional reality,
Just like all the rivers come and return to the ocean,
Along with the yanas, manifest and dissolve into buddha nature.
Therefore, this is called the ground Great Completion.

All the techniques and all the systems of practice mentioned above, like deities and mandalas, as well as all the spiritual vehicles, or yanas, are considered to be offspring of the tathagatagarba, or buddha nature, even though buddha nature itself is unconditioned.

Yet all these systems should be regarded as manifestations of the tathagatagarba as a means for our consciousness to be awakened to its buddha nature.

Since they are just conceptual systems as a means for awakening and are not permanent, eventually they will dissolve back into buddha nature, when one is no longer applying them. An analogy for this is like all the rivers returning to the great ocean. This returning can be experienced in deity yoga practices during the dissolution stage of the sadhana. One lets the whole mandala and all sacred forms dissolve into empty space for a while, which happens toward the end of the deity yoga practice. At this point, one might witness the great return of everything—the whole path—into buddha nature.

Ground Great Completion

Here, the verse also describes the ground *dzogpa chenpo* (W. *rdzogs pa chen po*), or the ground Great Completion. To comprehend this, it would be important to understand the very etymology of *dzogpa chenpo*, which is comprised of two words, *dzogpa* and *chenpo*.

Dzogpa means completion, which is stating that everything that exists in the realm of possibility, including samsara, nirvana, path, and so forth, are completely contained within dharmakaya awareness. This means everything is an expression of dharmakaya awareness. That is completion.

Great, or *chenpo*, means there is no higher Dharma than Dzogchen. (Dzogchen is an abbreviation of *dzogpa chenpo*.) This is perhaps the most standard definition of that etymology, but the definition is flexible, so other definitions are not mistaken. For example, in one of Dudjom Lingpa's revelatory writings, he said that *dzogpa,* or completion, means that the true meaning of all the nine yanas is complete. And *great* means it is the ground of all the vehicles. Ground Dzogchen is describing the primordial awareness in which all the enlightened qualities are not an effect of any cause but rather are always already complete in primordial awareness, even while one's consciousness is not enlightened.

Seeking the path of tirthikas is attachment to eternalism
and nihilism.
Due to clinging to appearances and experiences, the
mindstream is deluded in samsara.
The shravakas take selflessness of the individual
as the path;
The path of pratyekabuddhas reverses interdependent
origination and holds onto emptiness;
The Cittamatrins view all apparent existence as mind;
The Madhyamakins apprehend everything as emptiness;
The Kriya Yogis emphasize cleanliness and are
attached to objects;
The Upaya tantrikas mix the view of the upper and
lower tantras;
The Yoga tantrikas regard samayasattva and jnanasattva as
intrinsically separate.
Maha Yoga mistakenly perceives objects as real;
The path of Anu Yoga conceives space and wisdom as
cause and effect;
All their experiences and realizations of ground and paths
Are merely one speck of the spontaneous presence of
the Great Completion,
Like scooping water from the ocean and thinking
it is the ocean.
Realizing this, all other vehicles seem pitiful.

There is a hierarchy within all the spiritual systems even though they are all attempting to set us free. That hierarchy is not just invented but comes into being in relationship to how we naturally become enlightened. There is often a gradual process as we start the path and continue on it to become awakened. In that process, there is a stage where consciousness is very contracted, and then consciousness becomes more liberated until it is truly free. We can call this the spiritual growth of our consciousness. It can have many stages but just like other things, in the beginning, growth is limited, then it continues to mature. Therefore, the spiritual path has a hierarchy in that sense. In the beginning, the path is based on ideas, concepts, and methodology. In the end, these will all be transcended because our mind will outgrow all of them when it is ready to be fully awakened.

It would be mistaken to think that all the systems are useless or erroneous because they are part of duality from the point of view of Dzogchen. Here, the verses are not so much disparaging the other yanas but are pointing out their limitations.

Even though spiritual practices and philosophical systems are so numerous that they can never be counted, the mind continues proliferating them. Mind invents them with the motivation to understand life and the mystery of existence. The systems provide practices and methods for liberating the mind, and they establish ethical guidelines. Because they are developed by the mind, they always remain incomplete, and each has some hole or glitch, whereas the wisdom of Dzogchen goes beyond mind. It is not a mind-manufactured Dharma. Dzogchen transcends all *isms* in the purest sense.

In the Buddhist tradition, there are multiple ways to categorize spiritual and philosophical systems; many of these categories originated in India. One category is nihilism and eternalism. Nihilism is often described as a blunt denial of the law of cause and effect. Indeed, there have been philosophical tenets of nihilism even in ancient India. Eternalism refers to the schools of thought that Buddhism believes to be theistic, like those that hold the belief in an eternal self.

Buddhist Philosophical Systems

Even in Buddhism, there are philosophical systems and practices, such as the vehicle of the shravaka, which are incomplete because they are mind-based paths. Shravakas only meditate on no-self, and that method alone cannot lead to the realization of absolute freedom or the understanding of the complete nature of reality. They are considered the very beginners on the spiritual path.

The word *shravaka* literally means listeners, ones who listen to the spiritual teachings, the teachings of awakened ones. This indicates that they are students. They are usually described as not yet matured in the spiritual path, and their sole desire is to find freedom for themselves. They have not yet expanded their hearts to have the altruism that might inspire them to seek liberation for the benefit of others. They may be very diligent, become renunciates, and do serious practices like austerities, but it is usually all for themselves. The shravaka is usually described in Buddhist systems as an archetype of certain spiritual practitioners who are more focused on finding enlightenment for their own sake.

A little bit above the shravakas in the spiritual hierarchy are the pratyekabuddhas. Their system is also incomplete and cannot bring about complete awakening because pratyekabuddhas are lost in contemplation of the reversal of the twelve links of interdependent origination. The pratyekabuddha is someone who doesn't take anyone outside themselves as their spiritual teacher. There is a commonality between shravakas and pratyekabuddhas in that their whole quest is motivated by their desire to be free, but often the desire for seeking liberation for others is not part of their paradigm.

Even though the doctrines of Mahayana are considered not only advanced but very close to reality, from the Dzogchen point of view, they too have their own limitations. But the limitations can be very subtle. For example, the adherents of the mind-only school are trapped in a partial outlook on reality in which all things are only mind. They tend to assert that mind is real, and therefore they cannot transcend the mind. The Madhyamaka system is much more advanced and closer to the truth than the mind-only school, but they are still trapped by thinking that everything is empty. In this context, the emptiness they assert is part of the thinking mind, so it is another mental negation.

Tantric Systems

Even the tantric systems are incomplete and partial. Practitioners of Kriya Tantra are attached to a system that emphasizes physical cleanliness. This is because the outlook of Kriya Tantra is that the relationship between the deity and the practitioner is like the lord and a servant. Imagine that you are inviting the lord to your house. You would need to clean the house and wear presentable clothes.

Upaya Tantra is like a mixture of Kriya Tantra and Yoga Tantra. The view or doctrine is similar to that of the Yoga Tantra, but its observance, or conduct, is similar to that of Kriya Tantra. Traditionally this system has equal emphasis on meditation as well as physical observances. Yet the whole system is still a mind-manufactured system.

Yoga Tantra is a system that emphasizes inner meditation more than anything else, such as outer physical observances. Its fundamental outlook sees a separation between *samayasattva* and *jnanasattva*, as if they are two friends. Samayasattva is the form of the deity that is visualized by the practitioner in his or her mind. Jnanasattva is the actual deity, which is called bliss-empty awareness. It is not the form but the nondual awareness that corresponds to that form of the deity.

The next three tantric classes are often referred to as the inner tantras in the Nyingma system: Maha Yoga, Anu Yoga, and Ati Yoga. Maha Yoga is generally built upon the creation stage, utpatti-krama, whereas Anu Yoga is built upon the completion stage, sampanna-krama. The creation stage was already described earlier.

Completion Stage

The completion stage is a tantric practice often described as uncontrived yoga because it does not involve constructing something that is not already there, such as a deity mandala or form of a deity that we visualize in our mind. That form is not really in our natural being. Our mind creates the form during the creation stage while the completion stage, or sampanna-krama, utilizes our subtle body.

In Tibetan, the completion stage is called *dzog rim* (W. *rdzogs rim*). The word *dzog* means complete, indicating that something is already there, such as the subtle body, which is in us from the moment we are born. It's not something contrived. The subtle body is the psychophysiological system of nadi, prana, and bindu. Anu Yoga uses the subtle body to bring about a result, such as purification or awakening. This often involves using the power of meditation to bring the prana into the central channel, *avadhuti*, in order to produce awakening. This too is also somewhat conceptual and is still bound by its own system. Yet this is also considered completely contained within Dzogchen since Dzogchen is not lacking in anything.

To clarify, we might like to go back to an analogy in this verse. Dzogchen is described as the great ocean and all the other paths are like a small amount of the ocean's water. A scoop of water is not the complete ocean and yet all the water is completely contained in the ocean. In other words, one could say water is just part of the ocean. Therefore, Dzogpa Chenpo is an all-encompassing system that transcends all systems and at the same time, all systems are part of it. Once you realize the wisdom of Dzogchen, you realize the meaning of all the systems without having to go through each of them separately. If you only realize the meaning of these systems, you haven't yet realized the wisdom of Dzogchen.

Wisdom and primordial wisdom are actualized as the expanse of awareness.
Beyond accepting and rejecting, the Buddha Samantabhadra,
The essence of samsara, nirvana, and path, is the Great Completion.
Therefore, this is renowned as the path Great Completion.

We can synthesize the previous commentary into a concluding statement on the path Great Completion. How can there be a path Great Completion when everything is already complete in pure awareness, rigpa, or dharmakaya? The path Great Completion is not like any other kind of path. Here, the path is not separate from the ground Dzogpa Chenpo and fruition Dzogpa Chenpo.

That being said, in general, the path is a process involving methods to achieve a result, which is enlightenment. In the Dzogchen context, *path* refers to a method or process that allows one to experience a state in which all incidental display or phenomenal reality are dissolved into pure awareness. At the same time, in the realm of pure awareness, or rigpa, there is nothing to gain, nothing to purify. That state is the true Buddha Samantabhadra, which is the ground as well as the path. So the path is not separate from the ground.

This verse is radical because it transcends the path itself completely by referring back to the ultimate truth, which is the state of Samantabhadra, or rigpa, where there is nothing to gain, nothing to purify. That is the true path, the pathless path. And that is the path Great Completion.

All the causal vehicles boast of the fruition without achieving it.
Here, the actualization of buddha nature is Samantabhadra itself.
All the samsaric appearances and mind are self-liberated as kayas and wisdom
Without abandoning them. This is the authentic word of the buddhas.
Other than that, all the supposed fruitions of the other yanas are exhausting.
Therefore, this is the fruition of all Dharmas.
It is spontaneously present as the fruition Great Completion.

Yana is a Sanskrit word that generally refers to a spiritual path as well as the process of moving toward the great awakening. There are numerous ways of dissecting the groups of yanas. But here, the causal yana is mentioned, and the resultant yana is indicated. The causal yana is often known as Sutrayana, and the resultant yana refers to Vajrayana. The causal yana is the path tread by shravakas, pratyekabuddhas, and bodhisattvas. This division is because there is a fundamental difference between them.

There are a litany of reasons that describe how they are separate from each other even though their aim remains the same: to achieve enlightenment. But the simplest way to illuminate the demarcation between them is their speed. Sutrayana can be regarded as the slow path, and Vajrayana can be regarded as the fast path, or even a shortcut. It is like the difference between riding an ox to get somewhere versus riding *Mahabala*, the magical horse.

There are different interpretations of why Sutrayana is called the causal vehicle, but it is mainly because the process involves the effort of Dharma practices, which eventually allow one to experience enlightenment or buddhahood. Therefore, Sutrayana, or the causal vehicle, emphasizes that practice is done to cause enlightenment and doesn't consider the practices as enlightenment itself. Whereas Vajrayana allows one to become awakened swiftly. All along the path, it invites the individual to experience the result, the great fruition or enlightenment, through methods such as visualizing oneself as deity, embodying vajra pride, and resting in the awareness that one is already enlightened.

In Vajrayana, you are using a method that involves the result. You imagine you are the Buddha and you are enlightened. In that sense, we can say that the goal and the path are the same. Practitioners are encouraged to bring about buddhahood in the realm of now as opposed to thinking that everything they are doing will be the cause of enlightenment to be attained in the distant or near future but never right now.

In a general way, having different yanas is to be welcomed. It gives us permission to choose a path that works with our tendencies and personalities rather than feeling we are forced to take just one path whether it works for us or not. Imagine that the spiritual world is like a clothing or department store where there is only one type of jacket, color, style, and size. You might not find what you like—only a jacket that is too big or too small or doesn't suit you. Instead, we can think that the spiritual world is a clothing store with all the options of styles, colors, sizes, and so on. Having a variety of yanas is so wise, created with such good intention and kindness toward humanity. We are all so different from each other with our unique karmic tendencies.

This situation was mentioned in the famous legend about King Indrabodhi, who went to Buddha and asked for a path to enlightenment. Buddha said, "You need to become a renunciant," and the king refused such a suggestion. He told Buddha that was not possible for him. So it is said that Buddha taught him the path of Vajrayana. This is actually one of the best stories to illustrate why Vajrayana works for some people. It is said the reason King Indrabodhi didn't want to take the path Buddha recommended is because to be a renunciant you have to give up the pleasures of life, and the king had said he would not take any path where one had to abstain from or abandon pleasure.

In that respect, Vajrayana is not only considered the fastest path but also the path of non-rejecting. It doesn't reject light, and it doesn't reject darkness. It doesn't even reject neurosis or the delights of life. Because of this, Vajrayana is considered a path where you can be a true spiritual being, a yogi, or *tantrika*, while totally embracing life, which is so rich and diverse, filled with everything—beauty, sorrow, surroundings, relationship, moods, emotions, food, music, dance, conflicts, and more. Vajrayana doesn't encourage us to run away from aspects of life that seem unholy and to only cultivate the parts of life considered holy or wholesome.

There are indeed many images that symbolize the principle of Vajrayana. One is the vajra, and the other is the peacock, based on the myth that the more poison a peacock consumes, the more beautiful he becomes. This illustrates the premise of Vajrayana that even the dark side of life—like the kleshas, or inner poisons —doesn't have to be rejected or eradicated from one's own being. It can be embraced as part of the path, worked with skillfully, and used as fuel for enlightenment on the ground of nondual awareness. This principle is so important that sometimes Vajrayana indicates that if you are not in touch with your darkness, you won't become enlightened quickly.

For example, in Vajrayana, there are four tantras, as we mentioned. Each one is progressively more profound. It is said that people are ready to practice the highest tantra when things get really bad in the world, when people are confused. That is the time when people can practice the highest Vajrayana tantra, Anuttarayoga Tantra, of which Dzogchen is a part. Whereas an age when humanity is less conflicted is not considered the best time to practice the highest tantra. Lama Mipham said, "The darker the night gets, the brighter the lamp becomes." *Dark* here symbolizes a society that has become permeated with confusion, or a time when individuals are conflicted inside.

Dzogchen, The Direct Path

This verse is also saying that Vajrayana is more advanced in relationship to Sutrayana, and Dzogchen is the most direct path in Vajrayana. Even though riding Mahabala is used an analogy for the swift and dynamic path of Vajrayana, it can still be a complicated process. Perhaps you have to find a very fancy saddle and blanket, and you need to know how to ride. So even though it is a way to get someplace in a short time, it is complex. Whereas Dzogchen realizes you are already where you want to go, and you don't even need Mahabala. This makes everything much simpler.

On the path of Dzogchen, one begins with the realization of buddha nature, which is already residing in one's being as the nature of one's very own mind. Then through practice, that realization does not remain as an intellectual understanding but becomes a living experience, such that one will realize the highest level of enlightenment, the state of Buddha Samantabhadra, without waiting for it in a distant future. This is shown by the experience of many yogis who became enlightened in one lifetime. This is the unique characteristic of Ati Yoga. On this path, all the samsaric appearances as well as mental activities dissolve. Without abandoning anything or trying to achieve anything, one's consciousness will effortlessly be awakened as the mind of Buddha Samantabhadra. There is no higher state of consciousness to be attained.

Any path other than this path—such as looking for buddhahood and trying to achieve enlightenment through Sutrayana—can be exhausting. This is not just an intellectual statement but the experience of many people. When someone arrives at a level of truly understanding Dzogchen, he or she sees all the spiritual effort on other paths is exhausting because what they were searching for, such as buddhahood or nature of mind, was so close all along. It is already in each of us, according to Dzogchen. The dualistic paths will take us somewhere but will not take us where we really want to go. Not only that, these paths are filled with struggles. Some paths deliberately encourage us to struggle, often with the notion that enlightenment is very far away and separate from our life and ourselves.

Therefore, Dzogchen is already the result, the true fruition of all paths because it does not separate path and fruition. It invites us to experience the path as the goal as well as the result, or fruition. It is a nondual experience where there is no duality between path and goal, samsara and nirvana, and so forth. This totally nondual state is known as the fruition Great Completion.

Without falling into the extremes of existence and peace,
The great potential energy of knowledge and
primordial wisdom blazes.
Even though all these vehicles and their entrances
don't exist separately,
They are named for the benefit of those to be tamed.

True enlightenment is complete in itself. It transcends any limitations, known as extremes. In other words, it would not reside in any realm of samsara nor in any realm that is not fully liberated. There are two realms that are considered not fully enlightened: the realm of existence and the realm of peace.

The first realm is not physical but is a mental world of all beings who are completely under the power of unawareness, lost in their inner poisons, and stuck in the wheel of endless sorrow.

There are also spiritual beings, such as the shravakas and pratyekabuddhas, who may achieve their own version of nirvana, or deep peace, and unlike ordinary people, they are not troubled with their inner poisons. These beings have traveled the spiritual path practicing meditation and disciplines, but in achieving inner peace, they can sometimes get very attached to that peace. Often their attachment to their peace becomes a hindrance, and they lose any aspiration to mature their awakening to a higher level. In many ways, inner peace is a sublime state of mind where there is not as much suffering, but it becomes an obstacle to being fully awakened if one is attached to it. In general, shravakas and pratyekabuddhas are considered archetypical beings who are stuck in such peace.

This attachment to peace can also happen in our own spiritual practice, without even wearing the hat of a shravaka or pratyekabuddha. Often our spiritual practice comes with so much peace and joy that we can easily get attached to the bliss of peace and miss the most important spiritual aspects of compassion and altruistic engagement with the world. This is known as the "extreme of peace," which can take place regardless of what path or tradition one is practicing.

This can happen in Dzogchen practice, too, if one does not check their motivations as well as the quality of their own practice. I remember visiting a Buddhist community in North America where some long-term Dzogchen meditators lived. The place was very beautiful, in nature, far away from civilization, with very few grocery stores in the town. In conversation with someone, they made a humorous observation that the community was infected with a Dzogchen opioid crisis. The person was insinuating that some people in the community were practicing Dzogchen incorrectly. They were perhaps not getting anywhere on the Dzogchen path but instead got attached to some pleasant experiences from meditating in that beautiful environment where no one bothered them most of the time. There was humor in that observation as well as a warning.

Of course, Dzogchen itself is complete, full of love and compassion. Nothing is missing in Dzogchen, and it is free from all the pitfalls of other paths. But unless practitioners check their practice or consult with a wise teacher, they can end up being attached to bliss, thinking that is rigpa or Dzogchen, when it is actually far away from the real rigpa.

The true awakening of Dzogchen is complete. Nothing is missing: love, wisdom, compassion, courage, peace, and all the noble qualities are complete within it. Therefore, it is free from any of the so-called extremes, either an unawakened state of mind or incomplete nirvana.

In the realm of the absolute truth, there are no yanas, no stages of awakening, nor any practices and disciplines. These are merely conceptual categories. They don't exist in the realm of the absolute truth but are developed and taught by awakened masters only for the benefit of leading sentient beings to awakening. They are like the boat that helps others cross the river, but they are not the destination.

We must bear in mind that at some point, we should say farewell to the boat and arrive at the destination that is always here.

From the *Sharp Vajra of Awareness Tantra*, the fourth chapter on establishing the characteristic and quality of the ground.

V. Self-Liberation of Duality

Therefore, from the display of the great original purity,
The appearances and experiences of impure samsara arise.

There are things that we can conceive of, such as the concrete reality that is easily perceived by our senses of touch, smell, taste—our own body, houses, mountains, rivers, and so forth. Then there are things that are more conceptual and mental, like nirvana, enlightenment, and all the spiritual phenomena. We may sometimes wonder where they come from—are they the display of something that is utterly impersonal and transcendental? From the Dzogchen point of view, there is no omnipresent being that is a creator or source of all phenomena. Instead, Dzogchen teaches that all the phenomena that can be imagined in our consciousness are a miraculous display of *ka dag chen po* (W. *ka dag chen po*), the great original purity. This term is mainly found in Dzogchen writings and often means that original purity does not fall into any *lokas*, or realms, and cannot be categorized into nirvana or samsara.

Samsara and nirvana, the ordinary and the sacred, do not originate from separate sources. If they did, the logic would be depressingly dualistic; it would imply that there would be a permanent source of nirvana that is intrinsically good and an eternal source of samsara that is intrinsically bad.

So everything arises from the same source and dissolves into the same source. That source is the original ground. While the term *great original purity* is not as widely used in other Buddhist treatises as it is in Dzogchen, it is mentioned in other Buddhist writing. For example, the tathagatagarba and dharmadhatu are nothing other than this original purity. Tathagatagarba is buddha nature, but sometimes it is described as the source of all phenomena that we experience.

In his famous text *Uttaratantra*, Acharya Asanga stated that our personal experience of phenomena originally arises from buddha nature, which is none other than the pure luminous nature of one's own mind. In that passage, he used the traditional Indian cosmology:

Earth abides on water
Water abides on wind
Wind abides on space
Yet space does not abide on wind, water, or earth.

Likewise, the skandhas and dhatus (aggregates, elements, faculties) abide on kleshas and karma.
Karma and kleshas abide on mistaken conception.
Mistaken conception abides on the pure nature of the mind.
Yet, the pure nature of mind does not abide on any other phenomena.

This verse by Asanga is quite clear because it provides an image of how our own personal experience of reality arises from buddha nature. According to ancient Indian cosmology, this whole world is built upon layers of the different elements. First there is space, which has the characteristic of being unhindered, allowing everything to arise. From that, the other elements begin to arise. First is the wind, which has the ability to lift things up, to support and move things. Upon that, the water element comes into being, and from that, the earth was finally developed. Now you can see this kind of cosmology gives a clear picture that the world is built upon layers of elements, but the fundamental element is space. In that sense, space is the source and ground of all of them. They arise from space but space does not arise from them. Asanga wonderfully illustrated the correlation between this analogy and how all personal phenomena, including our body, samsaric consciousness, karma, and so forth, arise from buddha nature, which is like space.

Dzogchen and almost all the Mahayana schools describe a state from which everything arises, even though they might use different terms for it. In the Nyingma tradition, the tathagatagarba is also asserted as the source from which everything manifests. This is clearly stated in the most revered Nyingma tantra, the *Guhyagarbha Tantra*.

Even though original purity is beyond good or bad, one could regard this as a positive and benevolent theory. It gives the sense of reconnecting with a ground of everything that is utterly free, liberated, vast, and spacious, not bound by any conditions such as good or bad. Perhaps in the end, this is even better than saying everything comes from something that is good or exalted. Although our human mind has a tendency to be drawn to the good, the virtuous, and the exalted, the mind is still wandering in the limiting matrix of duality with these concepts.

One time after a meditation retreat in Asia, a group of us were traveling together in a car. One of the participants was sitting in the back seat, and he had some questions from the retreat. I had spoken quite a lot about the idea of *sacred* in that retreat. The person in the car asked me, "What is sacred?" We spent some time discussing it, then he said, "So there is no sacred. Sacred is a concept, right?" In that moment, I didn't really need to explain any more. I felt he understood the real sacred beyond the concept of sacred. He wasn't rejecting sacred but his question was resolved. He felt he understood it. There was a sense of freedom in that moment. The freedom came from dropping the idea of sacred, good, or sublime, which are still concepts. Any concept can be limiting and keep our consciousness from being truly free. So the idea of original purity is very liberating even though it doesn't hold any limiting notion like good, sublime, nirvana, and so forth. It is bigger than any of them.

Beyond Knowing and Not-Knowing

In general, our mind's relationship to reality is usually based on knowing and not-knowing. This is not an esoteric idea; when we feel we know something, that is knowing; and when we feel we don't know, that is not-knowing. This is true even in a casual situation. For example, if someone asks you, "Do you know so-and-so's phone number," if you know it, you would tell them yes and share it. But if you don't know, you say you don't know. That same mindset can be applied to theoretical matters, such as the mystery or origin of the universe, or the meaning of life. These are bigger, "heavy," metaphysical topics. Still, the mind is working through knowing or not-knowing. A scientist might say that she knows quite a lot about the origin of the universe and might tell you about the Big Bang theory. And she is pretty convinced that is an accurate theory of how the universe emerged and developed from the star novas into earth and the emergence of species, etc. But if you ask her what was happening before the big bang, she may say she does not know yet. The human mind has a desire to know, and often knowing is more comfortable than not-knowing.

But knowing is still a dualistic state of mind even if it is rational and accurate according to certain criteria. Not-knowing is also a dualistic state of mind, which comes with an uncomfortable feeling or doubt. In that sense, original purity has to be understood not in terms of knowing or not-knowing. This tells us that the ground or source of everything is beyond both knowing and not-knowing. To reside in that requires that we drop the usual *modus operandi* or strategy of the thinking mind. That may be the only way we can understand the true mystery of everything. In a Dzogchen prayer, Lama Mipham wrote,

> *Nothing is seen because it is beyond words and thought,*
> *Yet nothing remains that is unseen.*

Lama Mipham is saying that the original purity, or the absolute truth, is not something that can ever be known. The mind will never know it because there is nothing to know. It goes beyond words and thoughts, and mind usually knows something through its usual conceptual apparatus of words and thoughts. But it does not mean that we should be living in some existential fear or doubt about not knowing the nature of ultimate truth, or feeling that it is supposed to be there but we don't know it because it's beyond our mind. That feeling is uncomfortable, but Lama Mipham says that in such a profound awakening, do not stay with that uneasy feeling. Because in that moment, even though there is nothing to know, it's not like there is anything you don't know. The logic is that it goes beyond knowing and not knowing. There's no insecurity or fear because there is nothing that you are not knowing.

The subtle self-concept veils wisdom and insight.
While the inner glow and radiance of the ground settles in the womb,
The outer radiance is the undifferentiated base of samsara.
From that dead empty space, the aspect of clarity manifests.
The self-grasping consciousness arises as a base for experiences and appearances to unfold.
Only the mind itself exists as a potential basis for everything to arise.
From that, the six consciousnesses move.
Indefinite apparent objects appear as an illusory show.

From the undivided realm of original purity, the source of all, arises the unenlightened world of samsara. This happens because a very subtle self-concept emerges adventitiously from the realm of original purity, which is unhindered, spacious, and full of potential. The self-concept, *dak tok* (W. *bdag rtog*) emerges without any external factor simply because the ground is open for anything to emerge. This self-concept obscures the very nature of original purity and veils the primordial wisdom that knows the nature of reality. Due to that veiling, the inner radiance, *dang* (W. *mdangs*) of the primordial ground—or its enlightened dimension known as *kayas* and *jnanas*—goes into the womb of the undifferentiated state. *Kaya* is the enlightened form, and *jnana* is enlightened mind.

Here, kayas and jnanas should not be understood in a gross or tangible way. Kayas are, in general, associated with forms of deities and buddhas with particular characteristics such as colors, shapes, attire, and so forth. But here, kayas of inner radiance are not associated with deities with particular characteristics. In this context, kayas are dimensions from which enlightened forms can arise in our experience, such as forms of buddhas and their mandalas.

Now, due to this diversion from original purity, instead of awakening, unenlightenment takes place. Out of that situation, samsara manifests, which is the world of delusion. Then the external or outer radiance, *chi dang* (W. *phyi gdangs*), appears in the form of five colors. Out of that, all the perceived phenomenal world comes into being, including five elements and so forth. *Outer radiance,* a Dzogchen term used in this verse, means phenomena arise outwardly from the primordial ground. In this context, it is indicating that there is no recognition that such arising phenomena are the display of that ground.

This is also called the undifferentiated alaya, which is an unintelligent, dull state. It is not any particular state of mind and has no thoughts or emotions. In that sense, it is considered unintelligent, totally mindless, neither virtuous nor non-virtuous. This is known as alaya. As a reminder, the term *alaya* used in many Buddhist writings is not always the same concept. It needs to be interpreted in context.

From that alaya emerges mind-alone; there is no matter. That mind-alone has the attribute of being aware and intelligent. It also becomes the basis from which all other sensory consciousnesses come into being and engage with their own fields. For example, the eye consciousness engages with form, ear consciousness engages with sound, and so forth. Then the whole existence shines from that mind-alone as its own display. Not only do the sensory consciousnesses appear but even the seemingly physical phenomena arise, like colors, patterns, size, and shape. Because it is all a display of the mind itself, the perceived reality is not static; it has no stability but is in a state of constant fluctuation, just like mind itself. The entire phenomenal world arises, metaphorically speaking, like a magician's show. Yet alaya itself is not real and has no solid characteristics. It is just part of the whole illusion.

Without any stability, just like the tip of a hair is moved by the wind,
The five winds of manifestation, movement, separation, gathering, and transmutation
Cause formation, maintenance, destruction, and voidness of the eons.
The five sense-consciousnesses engage with perceived objects.
The movement of subtle consciousness arises as the perceiver, the subject.

The *prana*, or wind, plays a very important role. It not only moves the mind but also helps the entire existence come into being, making everything function in their own unique way. Even though the whole existence seems to be so solid to our perception —forms that we can see, consciousness that we can experience— the entire sensory world remains ephemeral, lacking in any solidity, like a hair blown by the wind. This analogy invites us to realize that the whole existence is unbelievably transient, with nothing to hold onto in the end. Not just our own life but the entire universe, the whole cosmos, is transient, no matter how vast and infinite it might appear. It is really not any more solid than your own life.

Buddhism often uses the eight metaphors of illusion, such as hallucination, mirage, dream, and so forth, to illustrate the transient nature of things These metaphors indicate the same thing as this analogy of the movement of a hair tip. They point out that not only are insignificant things transient—like a flower in your garden, snow on the roof of your house—but the entire cosmos fundamentally rests on nothing. Everything is changing in every millisecond and things have no intrinsic reality. Yet they exist with their own functions and their own life. The universe itself is alive. When you look around, everything has its own life.

In this context, the entire existence is run by the forces known as the pranas, or literally, winds. This verse gives us the category of the five pranas. It states that the wind of manifestation allows everything, all phenomena, to arise from empty space. The wind of movement allows all things to appear in any possible fashion and in numerous forms. The wind of separation allows things to be unique and not mixed together. For example, water and fire are each distinct from each other. The wind of gathering holds everything together. The last one is the wind of transmutation, which allows the destruction of everything.

In general, the five pranas appear in tantric treatises as well as in Tibetan medical science, but the categories are not always the same, and their meaning is interpreted in different ways. For example, in Tibetan medicine, the five pranas are the forces that run our life, and without them, our life would not function. Like fuel for a motor, these five pranas can be regarded as fuel for our life, with functions like breathing, digesting, etc. In the same way, the five pranas mentioned in this verse are like the fuel for the whole existence to come into being in the first place and to be alive, in constant motion, changing, expanding and contracting, creating and destroying, and so on. The Big Bang and black holes could be said to be propelled by these pranas, according to the Vajrayana doctrine.

So the movement of one's life and the whole universe is happening within the three principles of formation, sustenance, and destruction. These three principles of life are commonly held notions in many traditions in the East. They also correspond to a *kalpa*, or eon. *Kalpa* means time or eon. There are four kalpas known as formation, maintenance, destruction, and voidness. This is also a common concept held in Buddhist literature, which says the world comes into being, self-destructs, and remains for a period of time as empty space. Then it emerges again.

Countless subtle eons dissolve even within one day.
Entering into the sphere of the mind is the waking state.
Entering into the sphere of alaya is the sleeping state.
When moving toward sleep, an eon of time dissolves into space.

Every moment is like an eon because every moment has its own form of the three principles of formation, maintenance, and destruction. Yet the idea of an eon is totally a state of our mind, because time is not solid. Not only that, in the ultimate sense, time does not exist. It is purely a mental construct. That's why in the Nyingma Tantras, time is divided into four: past, present, future, and no-time. A short time or long time is a subjective experience.

There is a folk story in Golok which says that before you go to bed, you need to put your cup upside down because during the night an entire world of spirits, or *gandharvas*, can form in the cup, and in the morning, using the cup would destroy their world. It is a folk story that has some wisdom, saying that the duration of time is just a subjective experience. The folk story says that for some beings, one night could be a whole eon where their world can form, be sustained, and be destroyed. The wisdom is that everything including time is our own perception, and the world is more transient than we think.

Each day in our own experience is a kalpa in itself. It starts in the early morning; then when the sun goes down and we fall asleep, it is the end of the day. That day will never return, so the world that existed that day collapses in that very moment. The concept of kalpa can be applied to any amount of time, from the infinitesimal to the infinite.

This is a perspective that sees a day as a lifetime. Every night when we go to bed, it's almost as if we are taking a long break from life. Hopefully, everybody will have a good sleep, a wonderful period when you can just let go of all your thoughts. You have no more responsibilities and you can just fall asleep with a sense of ease and comfort.

The next day when you wake up in the early morning, it is like the beginning of a whole new life. You wake with a lot of curiosity about the unknown because you don't really know what kind of situation you are going to encounter during the day. It often seems that every day is under our control, and we can decide what to do and what not to do. But actually, that's a little bit of an illusion. Every day is full of surprises because no one really knows exactly how the day is going to unfold.

Basically, this verse is about changing our idea of a day or of time. In this context, it is to see every day as a whole lifetime. When you wake up, it would be powerful to feel that you are newly born in this world and let go of the belief that you have control over your life or that you know what is going to happen. Instead, welcome the day with the sense of not knowing and also with curiosity, anticipating all the unfolding unknowns and surprises in the day. You hold the intention and aspiration that you are going to welcome the day and every surprise, not with fear, not with anger, but with an open heart, courage, love, and equanimity. The point is that we have the choice each moment to be in awareness or at least in a state of equilibrium regardless of what is happening. All these Buddhist teachings are pointing out that there is always a state of our mind where we can reside and where we will not be challenged by whatever is happening around us or within us.

When the mind and senses engage with their own field, our experience is the waking state during the day. At night, there is a process of falling asleep, where our five senses and mind dissolve into alaya consciousness, which dissolves into alaya.

Alaya and Alaya Consciousness

Alaya, *kunzhi* in Tibetan, and alaya consciousness, *kunzhi namshe*, are separate dimensions with very subtle differences. In theory, alaya is like a mindless, unintelligent state that has the capacity to store all the karmic imprints. Whereas alaya consciousness has the ability to be aware of itself, and it has some kind of intelligence.

The best way to understand them is to bring them into our personal experience. Longchenpa wrote a very clear description of the demarcation between the two. He said, for example, imagine that someone is completely physically exhausted. When you rest in that state, there is a moment when nothing is going on in your mind. That is alaya. Then in a short time, your mind becomes aware of what is happening around you, you come to your senses, and you become aware of yourself. You begin to feel you are no longer in a mindless state: that is alaya consciousness. Then you begin to hear sounds clearly and see forms clearly as the other sensory consciousnesses arise.

Let's revisit this example. Imagine you are running up a hill, carrying a heavy bag. If you don't stop at all and you get a little dehydrated, at some point you can't go any further, and you have to stop. You almost feel like you will faint. In that moment, your senses are not there, the mind is not operating, and you are so tired, it is almost like being unconscious. That is the alaya state. After a while, you feel you are coming back to your senses. That is the alaya consciousness. Then your senses start working well. You look around at the mountain and see where you are. People are talking, cows or sheep are making noises, you may feel sensations of the sunlight or wind on your skin. These are the sensory consciousnesses.

There are many moments in our life when we are descending into alaya, such as falling asleep. During the sleeping process, there is a moment when the conceptual mind is no longer there and is totally blacked out. The only thing that remains is alaya, the unintelligent state of mind. When dreaming begins, even though it is totally mental, a world and reality begins. Therefore, every night when we go to sleep, an entire eon is dissolved into empty space.

It's not that difficult, therefore, to relate to the use of the word *kalpa* as one of the four kalpas that contains countless human ages. It is also used to capture the state where each moment, each hour, each day, is a complete kalpa in which a world comes into being and eventually dissolves. It may be hard to relate to this use of kalpa in everyday life, but it makes sense when you think of the process of waking each morning, going to bed at night, and a whole kalpa comes to an end.

This idea is also applicable if we are meditating on the cushion, for example. When we come out of meditation, there is a big energetic shift, as if we left one reality and entered another one. It's like meditation was an eon and then when we come out, an entire new eon begins because of the contrast between the state of mind while one is meditating and not meditating.

Alaya exists as the formless realm, klesha consciousness exists as the form realm,
Mind itself spontaneously exists as the realm of desire.
The three worlds do not exist outside; not even one speck of dust.

The same logic about kalpas can apply not only to time but to dimension. For example, think about the entire world system. Buddhism teaches there is no specific number of worlds that exist in the universe. It is limitless; the texts say wherever there is space, there is a world. There is also a world system taught in the *Kalachakra Tantra* and Abhidharma, such as the three-thousand-fold world system, which is our galaxy. There are also many galaxies besides ours according to Buddhist cosmology. When we say *world,* usually we are referring to the greater system that involves planets, mountains, rivers, stars, sun, and moon. At the same time, there are infinitesimal worlds.

For example, our own house could be a world in itself, just like a cup can be a whole world for the gandharavas. Our house has a boundary between its inhabitants and what lies beyond it. Sometimes we feel we are part of the outside world, and sometimes we are so settled in our own house, we forget there is a whole world outside, especially when we spend a lot of time at home. Then we feel our house is the whole world. If you are relatively happy and content, you feel your world is quite benevolent. But if your mind is going crazy with all its neurotic thoughts, you feel your world is troubled.

As human beings, we all live in the same world collectively, and we don't each have our own private moon to gaze at. There is only one moon and millions of people are staring at the same beautiful bright moon that we are seeing. But at the same time, we are living in our own world. Our house becomes a galaxy, and we experience our own reality, including our thoughts, emotions, moods, and interpersonal relationships with our family members.

So the verse says that the whole world that appears in your own consciousness is your own perception. The world that you see is a display of your own consciousness. In that sense, what is known as the three spheres in Buddhism—realm of desire, realm of form, and realm of formlessness—are each a reflection of your own mind. For example, the realm of formlessness is a reflection of the alaya; the realm of form is a reflection of klesha consciousness, and the world of desire is a reflection of the mind. *Klesha consciousness* is a consciousness that observes alaya consciousness and identifies with it as "I am."

From that point of view, nothing else truly exists other than as merely reflections of our own consciousness. This understanding is very radical and contrary to our ordinary, day-to-day perception of reality. But this radical understanding is closer to the truth than any belief system or perception we might have that is based on our ordinary mind. As human beings, we always trust our ordinary thinking mind but that is a problem. We have a strong resistance to questioning what we see or believe. Then, when our belief systems develop a crack, we may start to question them, but there is still an idea that our senses are valid.

But our senses are not valid either, and the falsity of the senses can be easily proven. For example, if you put a stick into water, the stick looks quite big or bent, but it is not really so. Buddha said, in the *Samadhiraja Sutra:*

Eyes, ears, nose, are not valid.
Tongue, body, mind are also not valid.
If these faculties are valid,
What is the use of the path of the noble ones?

Buddha is basically saying that even our perceptions and sensory experiences are not completely reliable. They cannot be used as an infallible tool to determine what is true and false, what is real and what is unreal. Obviously the world of Buddha's mind and the world of a sentient being's mind are quite different. Buddha's mind and a sentient being's mind also perceive reality differently. Buddha's mind perceives that there is no intrinsic reality, and everything is empty of svabhava, or intrinsic nature. The mind of sentient beings sees everything as real, solid, separate, and divided.

So the question is, which one would win if there were a trial between them? Imagine that truth is on the side of the Buddha's mind. Even though there might be a lot of convincing arguments from sentient beings, they would be proven false because they don't have truth on their side. Chandrakirti said something similar in *Madhyamakalamkara.* He said:

The perception of the eye that is jaundiced
never can refute the eye that is free of such a disease.
Likewise, the mind that is devoid of stainless wisdom
cannot refute the stainless wisdom mind.

Buddhism employs this logic to tell us that even though the absolute truth—emptiness, all-pervasive sacredness, nonduality—is hard for the mind to comprehend, in the end we must see the falsity of our own perceptions and belief systems, and rise above the known world of our mind. Then we can awaken to the absolute truth, which is the opposite of our normal perceptions.

Even the idea that nothing exists outside our consciousness, which is the crux of Mahayana and Vajrayana traditions, is extremely difficult for our day-to-day mind. But such truth can be discovered either through deep, thorough inquiry, or through other radical means taught in the Vajrayana traditions.

The Rudra of self-view is the Matramkah of samsara.
Your body exists as the realm of desire, your speech is the realm of form,
Your mind exists as the four formless absorptions.
Your flesh, blood, heat, breath, white and red bindu, and essence,
Exist as the four elements, sun, moon, Rahula, and so forth.

The main root of samsara as well as most suffering that exists in our life is found within our mind. In other words, the root of samsara is a state of consciousness. This fact becomes more and more obvious as we engage with deep inquiry into the very foundation of all our *dukkha*, which is the Buddhist term for universal suffering. The root of samsara is self-view, or *dak ta* (W. *bdag lta*), which is an ingrained, firmly developed belief that there is a separate self that is truly who we are, and we are attached to it. This is the basis on which samsara is developed.

Therefore self-view is portrayed not as a benevolent being but as a malevolent being, Rudra, who is an absolute troublemaker. Among all the troublemaking characters in the Tantric Buddhist literature, the greatest would be Rudra. The tantras sometimes mention eight kinds of Rudra, including Matramkah Rudra, who is absolutely evil, powerful, and has an uncontrollable desire to subdue everyone and conquer more realms. He is the scariest, most monstrous character in all of Tantric Buddhist liturgies. But bear in mind that he is not invincible. Who is he? He is not really an entity. He represents the mind that reifies objective reality and lives in the mind of unenlightened beings.

There is an elaborate legend about him, which is entertaining as well as meaningful and filled with significance. It says that Rudra was a powerful being with a mighty retinue whose task was to create hindrances for individuals on the spiritual path. Vajrasattva decided it was time to tame Rudra and invited the Buddhas from the ten directions to a "conference" on how to tame him. Out of that conference, a glorious Heruka manifested. While Rudra was away, Heruka went to Rudra's kingdom and consecrated it as a sacred world. When Rudra returned, he saw that his kingdom was now a mandala, got extremely frightened, and uttered his own mantra, *Rulu, Rulu, Rulu*. In that moment, Heruka consecrated that mantra into a sacred mantra. Then Heruka subdued Rudra, blessed him as a Dharma guardian named Mahakala, and transformed his consciousness. Heruka prophesied that Mahakala would become fully enlightened in the future.

As you read these stories, they are kind of frightening if you think that no one can stop this being. But this legend tells us that the *herukas*, the wrathful Buddhas, are more powerful, which gives us the hope that the light always wins. This story has another significance. It is about the inner transformation of our consciousness from being deluded to being fully awakened. As we mentioned, Rudra is the dualistic mind that reifies everything. The liberation of Rudra is the liberation of the mind.

So this verse states that the impure physical world is a creation of this Rudra, or self-view. Earth is his flesh, water is his blood. Fire is his body-heat, and the wind is his breath. His white and red bindu are the sun and moon, and his essence is the planet Rahula. The point is that as long as we are unenlightened, our experience of the whole world is tainted by the self-view, which causes endless suffering.

But this does not mean that the world is intrinsically impure. The verse is saying that if we perceive the world by identifying with the separate self, then the world is filled with suffering. But if we can embrace the world from another state of consciousness, enlightened consciousness, then the world is already pure and sacred.

This view of a sacred world is the primary doctrine of Vajrayana. For example, Vajrayana treatises establish the ten principles of tantra, and the first one is called the view, or the fundamental outlook of Vajrayana. In the Nyingma tradition, the tantric view is that not only is the ultimate truth pure but even the relative truth is pure. They use the term *exalted relative truth,* which is radical because *exalted* is usually associated with the absolute. But *exalted relative truth* means that even samsara is pure if you are able to embrace it with enlightened mind.

This notion of exalted relative truth is wisdom that is so needed in today's world, where the fundamental view of the world and nature is materialistic, in which everything seems meaningless and all things are merely objects. It is not just the natural world that is perceived through such a view; even people and also their bodies are regarded as objects. The result is disastrous. It leads the entire society to degrade the environment as well as to objectify each other. In this way, so much harm can be caused.

It is not only modern materialism that has this problem. Orthodox religions also have this problem when they create a duality between sacred and secular, holy and unholy, pure and impure. The nondual view, the exalted relative truth, can bring about so much healing to the world by restoring reverence to everything. Then the relationship between people, and between nature and people, can become a bond that serves as a universal healing.

The sharp vajra of no-self
Liberates [Rudra] by its power and splendor, and in the pure expanse,
The subtle enlightened body and great primordial wisdom are actualized.
Without abandoning samsara, the liberation of buddhahood [occurs].
Without abandoning self-view, everything dissolves into the display of spontaneous presence.

An important expression in Vajrayana, *liberation*, or in Tibetan, *dral wa* (W. *bsgral' ba*), has a very specific meaning. It has the connotation of a radical or forceful liberation. When our unenlightened mind is resistant to awakening, it seems that a powerful force is required to liberate it. This kind of powerful force is expressed in the legend of Rudra, where Rudra is the epitome of unawareness, the very force that binds us to samsara.

The Heruka, according to the legend, had to forcefully liberate Rudra's mind. The true meaning of *heruka* is nondual wisdom, the wisdom of no-self, which liberates our unenlightened mind from the trap of self-view. Radical, nondual liberation is a profound awakening that comes from realizing that samsara does not exist in the first place and there is nothing to be liberated. According to the nondual view of Vajrayana, there is no real samsara and the true nature of reality is already enlightened from the very beginning, if one can only see it.

Some Buddhist doctrines hold that samsara is outside of ourselves, nirvana also lies outside of our consciousness, and that samsara and nirvana are two diametrically opposed, contradictory sides of life. Vajrayana teaches that the world and life are not samsara. Samsara only comes into being when our mind is veiled by the fundamental ignorance that does not see the enlightened nature of all things. So samsara is purely a state of mind. In a dualistic point of view, samsara is held as something to be rejected and nirvana is something to be attained. This is built on a dualistic matrix of attaining and rejecting. Here we are transcending the idea of rejecting. There is no rejecting, there is nothing to be rejected, and there is also nothing to be obtained. As the *Heart Sutra* says, "there is no attainment, no non-attainment."

In the awakening that sees that all things are already enlightened, samsara is already dissolved, and nirvana is already here and has been here from the beginning. This liberating truth is not the domain of our ordinary intellect. It is a living truth that one can taste in the realm of nonconceptual mind.

From the *Sharp Vajra of Awareness Tantra*, the fifth chapter on establishing the secret duality of subject and object, and the way that self-liberation occurs.

VI. Revealing Clear Distinctions and Vital Points of the Practice

Now calling upon the actual Buddha of the primordial ground as a witness,
Generating the power of pure aspiration,
Commit to the buddhahood of omniscience.

This chapter deals with different topics and begins with an aspiration prayer of setting an intention. An aspiration prayer is a huge part of all the paths within the Buddhist tradition but the nature of the prayers varies in different contexts. For example, aspiration prayers in accordance with Hinayana and Mahayana are distinct from each other, and their underlying intention may not be the same.

Aspiration prayers come with specific intentions. An aspiration prayer is a powerful means for enhancing our intention to actualize what we are seeking—the ultimate awakening. In the Buddhist tradition, a practitioner imagines inviting a whole host of deities, buddhas, and bodhisattvas. In the Mahayana tradition, one might visualize the one thousand buddhas of the fortunate eon or the eight bodhisattvas, and then engage in an aspirational prayer with a specific intention. Similarly, a tantrika would beckon to mind the gurus, ishtadevatas, and dakinis as witnesses for the aspiration prayer.

This verse indicates that we invite not just any buddhas or bodhisattvas but the ultimate, highest buddha, the Primordial Buddha, which is the Dharmakaya Buddha. That buddha lies within each of us and is none other than the true nature of our consciousness, which is already pure and luminous. So there is no duality in this invitation of a witness, as we are the inviter and the Primordial Buddha is the invitee. What we are inviting is already within.

In general, there is a power from inviting a witness whenever we set an intention before embarking on any endeavor, whether it is spiritual or secular. Our commitment tends to take root more deeply in our mind. This is why in many spiritual and religious traditions, people often mentally invite a witness, either a living person or a sacred principle, when they make vows and set intentions. This is true even with cultural practices and rites; for example, at wedding ceremonies, people invite their most beloved parents, cousins, brothers, sisters, nieces, nephews, and friends as witnesses for their sacred union. There is a reason why people do this—perhaps the commitment will last longer because it was sanctified by all the witnesses that they love or respect. Therefore here, in the context of this tantra, you can use the idea of inviting a sacred witness in conjunction with studying and practicing this text.

This chapter presents a group of practices and recommends that we begin all these practices by setting an intention in the form of an aspirational prayer. The prayer here is to hold the wish and the vow to become enlightened. In other words, to return to the primordial ground. This is a critical component of all Buddhist practice, without which there could be a disconnect between one's intention and the practice itself, and then the practice would end up not having much impact.

The aspiration prayer can be done in silence. You could also choose an existing liturgy that is congruent with the following practices or even compose your own prayers, which can be used at the beginning of the practices. You could say, for example, "I invite Buddha Samantabhadra as a witness. I shall become enlightened and awakened to the true nature of my consciousness through this practice that I am about to engage with." You can offer a prayer of whatever arises in your mind as long as the content of the prayer goes along with the teaching.

At all times, training in dying, and drawing in and uniting,
It is important to practice their essential points.

This list of practices begins with training in dying, or in Tibetan, *chi* (W. *'chi*). It is said that one who is truly awakened does not need such a practice, yet it would be very useful for many people to prepare for the journey of dying right now regardless of their age or health situation. It is simply a matter of time; eventually, everyone will die as part of nature's cycle. But there is a way to die consciously so that dying would not be filled with fear and confusion.

Many societies do not invest in any kind of spiritual education about this topic although all religious traditions have doctrines about what exists beyond this life. But even with that, they may not have an entire training or set of meditations on how to die consciously. This may sound mystical or esoteric, but it is not. Instead, it is very practical and sensible, and it is a very big part of Vajrayana

There are often conversations about how to live, because living is a big part of life. Living has different rites and stages from youth to old age, such as getting educated, married, and fulfilling one's role in the world. Dying, like any of these stages, is also a very important part of life. At the same time, it may not be a fun topic to talk about. It may be a bit taboo in certain cultures because it is related to the possibility of the demise of our existence. This can be scary as well as the ultimate humiliation to our ego when we realize nature has the upper hand. Dying tells the ego that we will lose everything that we cherish or are proud of. Many cultures may not have spiritual practices that give a more enlightened perspective on dying and death, and how to work with these stages.

This training in dying is more than just learning how to die peacefully. It is about how to become enlightened during that process. The reason to have training for dying is that the process of dying is an unknown territory for our mind. It is a moment when the body is shutting down, and perhaps many people would lose their usual mental capacity; some people may also go through confusion and discomfort. It is also perhaps difficult to have awareness during the dying process. Even if someone is a well-seasoned meditator, he or she could lose remembrance, forgetting to meditate and maintain awareness during that period.

There are numerous practices in Vajrayana on death and dying that enable us to die consciously with peace and to rest in the luminous nature of mind, or pure awareness. These techniques can turn the whole process of dying into another doorway to awakening.

Practice Instructions for Dying

There are specific practices on the training for dying that can be found in other texts, but here is a summary of them. The practice begins by working with a posture known as the pose of a lion lying down, which is lying on the right side, supporting your cheek with your right hand and your left hand on your thigh. When dying you may be lying on a bed, and the lion represents the king of the jungle, giving the sense that you are fearless and totally confident on this journey. It is said that many meditation masters died in this posture. Posture is important because if someone remembers to take a posture while dying, they are already prepared to die consciously. Without such awareness, one wouldn't even remember to take the posture. So posture, awareness, intention, and preparation all go together.

Not only spiritual masters but even great warriors have the mental prowess to die with dignity. For them, dying is such an important part of their life and perhaps their whole path is to end life with the dignity of a warrior. They may not die in a meditative state, but they don't want to leave the world without the dignity that they were steadfastly upholding all their life. For example, one of the greatest Japanese swordsmen was Miyamoto Musashi. He won every duel that he engaged in. He also wrote *The Book of Five Rings*, his guide on leadership. It is said that when he was dying, he picked up his sword to help himself sit up, put his sword on the ground, and died in a hero's posture. He died with dignity as a hero. The point is that even without bringing spirituality into the topic, with some kind of preparation, people can die with whatever their intention is—peace, dignity, or perhaps enlightenment. All this reminds us that many people have the ability, if they want to use it, to die in a certain way based on their intention.

In Tibet, many meditation masters die with conscious preparation. Sometimes they put on their beautiful monastic robes, letting everyone know they are ready to die. Then they sit in a cross-legged meditation posture and die consciously while meditating in rigpa, or pure awareness. This is so common in Tibet that it is hard to give just one example. It is not just a rare story of only a few spiritual masters of the past. Even today you hear that many yogis in Tibet die consciously after taking a specific posture.

After taking the lion's posture, then imagine you are directing your consciousness to your eyes instead of other parts of your body. For a regular meditator, this should be quite easy since meditators are trained to direct their attention to objects such as the breath. Next, allow yourself to direct your eyes into empty space, and rest and relax without trying to modify or manipulate your experience. Then abide with ease in the expansiveness and spaciousness that arises when the mind is no longer caught up in any thoughts.

This practice allows one to experience that one's awareness is enlightened because the sense of self, the "I am," dissolves. In Dzogchen, there is an emphasis on expanding your awareness. When your awareness expands, your thoughts and mental events no longer dominate your mind. Instead, there is a direct recognition of the luminous nature of mind. So the postures and practices were developed to expand one's awareness.

That state of mind is called dharmakaya mind, which is the pure, original nature of mind. Sometimes this is also called naked awareness. It is like your consciousness is stripped of all the trappings of internal conditions, such as all the kleshas, ordinary thoughts and emotions, and so on. In other words, your consciousness is not bound by any of them, including the ego—your consciousness is not associated with ego at all in that moment. This is very powerful. In its essence, consciousness is already pure and enlightened, but it is wrapped up in trappings of internal conditions, often created by unawareness. This practice is a training to experience this naked awareness at the time of dying.

You can train in the practice again and again, which will give you the confidence to stay in the same kind of expansive, spacious state of mind when the process of dying happens. Then life ends with enlightenment. It is the best grand finale for your life's journey.

Drawing in and Uniting

The following practice, "drawing in and uniting," *ba wa* (W. *sba ba*) and *du* (W. *bsdu*), is done at night.

At dusk, one sits in the posture of a sage and visualizes, in the belly, a red lotus with four petals, in the middle of which is a red-hot *ah-shed* symbol, described earlier as resembling a narrow triangle wider at one end. From this, fire ignites, travels through the central channel up to a *hang* (ཧཾ) letter in the crown chakra. Nectar descends that feeds the fire, which burns all one's karma and karmic patterns in one's system. Then one rests in what is called bliss-empty awareness.

When you are ready to fall asleep, sit in the posture of a sitting elephant and visualize the *Ah* (ཨ) letter in the heart center in the central channel, above which are twenty more *Ah* letters stacked in a vertical column radiating light everywhere. Eventually they all dissolve one after the other into the original *Ah*. Meditate in that state until falling asleep naturally.

In the morning, practice the three-breaths purification—three deep inhalations and exhalations—expelling the stale prana while saying *Hah.* From a white *Ah* (ཨ) syllable in the heart, radiate another white *Ah* syllable, about twenty finger-widths in the space above and in front of the eyebrows. Concentrate on that for a while. From that syllable radiates an immeasurable number of light rays, which reflect upon the entire world of sentient beings including oneself. All the suffering and karma of the whole world is suddenly purified. Then you and the whole world dissolve into light, which dissolves back into the *Ah* syllable. Rest in nonconceptual awareness. Once you get up, remember to be mindful, and live in that nonconceptual awareness as much as possible throughout the whole day in all situations.

Benefit of These Practices

These practices are complete in themselves, in that they can be integrated into major and minor aspects of life. Even though life has numerous events, periods, and stages, in some sense they are all happening in the framework of the dying, sleeping, and waking states. Each day we wake up, and everything that takes place while we are awake—whether engaging with spiritual practices or completely involved in ordinary affairs—is all part of the waking state. And each day, we fall asleep, usually at night, and that too is part of our daily life. The sleeping state is often unconscious, but it may also involve dreams and has its own life.

In the end, dying comes to everyone as an exit from this world. In Tibetan Buddhism, death is sometimes called the great migration, which is a poetic way of describing it. Sometimes the word *death* is associated with a negative meaning and may even be part of a curse, like "Death to…". But saying *great migration* changes our notion of death. It is something we can relate to because we often move around from one town to another, one country to another. We would have a hard time reciting off the top of our heads all the zip codes of places where we lived. *Great migration* says death is not death in the ultimate sense; it is not a nihilistic version of the total end of your being.

These practices are a way to maintain awareness and not be lost in our thoughts and emotions, either while awake or while falling asleep. They can be done either for a long period of time or a short period, such as months or weeks, until there is a tangible result. These practices can enable someone to go through a very profound inner transformation, feeling that he or she is free from karmic and mental chains. They give a practitioner confidence about how to live and how to die in the realm of awareness without becoming totally deluded.

If you don't get any of these results, the practices will at least help you to not get lost in the usual thinking mind, which is constantly chattering. That chattering mind produces anxiety, worry, judgement, and so forth. This is the state of mind in which many people in the world live without knowing that there is another state of mind. So anything that helps us to have even a temporary break from that noisy mind is worthwhile.

It is possible someone can have an extraordinary transformation by trying these practices on their own. However, they can be even more powerful when done with guidance. In general, it would be appropriate to take oral teachings on the text from a living teacher who would offer guidance, including one-on-one dialogue, and taking the practitioner step by step. In that way, one would experience the full benefit of these practices, which are designed to produce a very powerful awakening in one's consciousness.

The heart of the realization from these practices is more than just knowing how to approach the next stage of your journey but to come to the radical realization that there is no one who dies. You realize you are no longer a separate entity that has a beginning and an ending, but your true nature is the unborn, deathless, Primordial Buddha.

The actualization of the expanse of alaya is the
dharmakaya Samantabhadra.
The actualization of the expanse of mind-consciousness is
the great wisdom.
The actualization of nature of mind is the supreme
path of awareness.
From the actualization of consciousness, the potential
energy of primordial wisdom blazes.
The actualization of the nature of sentient beings
is the Buddha.
Exhaustion of impure appearances and experiences
is true liberation.
Arriving at the understanding of the natural state
is realization.
Likewise, without being ignorant of the vital point
of clear distinctions,
It is important to strike the vital points of the practice.

There are pitfalls on the path in general, whether Vajrayana or Dzogchen. These traditions come with a system that provides a map pointing out these pitfalls, reminding us to be aware of them. Otherwise, one can fall into them, often mistaking samsaric, mundane states of mind as enlightened mind or pure awareness. Sometimes these pitfalls appear on the surface as something other than what they really are. In that way, one can easily misconstrue the false as the real.

Imagine you are embarking on a long journey, and suddenly there is a crossroad. If you are a bit sleepy, misread the sign, and keep walking, you will not get to the destination. You may never wake up and realize you are on the wrong track. Or you do wake up and see how much time was wasted. Therefore, it would be good to read some kind of guidebook before starting on the journey, which warns you ahead of time of the crossroads where such mistakes can occur.

The instructions about the pitfalls are called *shen jé* (W. *shan 'byed*), or distinctions. These distinctions are a well-known topic in the Dzogchen texts. They are not obscure at all. Many Dzogchen masters wrote a great deal about this topic.

Alaya and Dharmakaya

The first distinction is distinguishing between alaya and dharmakaya. Alaya is a term used throughout Tantric Buddhist scriptures, yet its meaning varies so one should interpret this term in context. Here, alaya is the unintelligent ground on which our ordinary samsaric mind, thoughts, emotions, and karmic patterns arise. It is the ground where our karmic habits are stored.

A traditional analogy to describe alaya is to think of water. The nature of water is pristine, clear, and drinkable. Unpolluted water is a beautiful image in our mind. It invokes a sense of purity, cleanliness, and beauty. When water is so pristine, it can even act as a reflecting mirror. Drinking or even observing clean water is also pleasing to the senses. Then imagine that this water is polluted by mud. When the water is no longer pristine, it loses all its lovely attributes in our perception. Yet it is still the same water.

Our human consciousness is like water. In the same way that the nature of water is pristine, the nature of our consciousness is already pure, free from all karmic conditions. Alaya is like that muddy water. The mud represents original ignorance that obscures the pristine quality of consciousness. Whereas dharmakaya, the nature of consciousness, is like unpolluted water, pristine, pure, drinkable. Dharmakaya, which is the highest state of buddhahood, is like water that is free from mud. Dharmakaya is a state of consciousness that is free from all internal conditions. It is consciousness being what it is. Dharmakaya is not some supreme quality newly added to consciousness but is its natural state.

Nirvana and samsara are two different states of consciousness —there is no doubt about that. One is totally liberated and the other is imprisoned in its own delusions. But it is not that there is a huge, physical distance between them, such as between sky and earth. They are different states of the same consciousness, like clear water and muddy water, even though to our mind, it feels like there are thousands of metaphysical miles between them. We feel the only way to get to nirvana is by leaving samsara behind. Not only that, it seems that the distance is really far, the path zigzags and the journey might be adventurous, with towns and villages along the way that are mini-nirvanas, resting stations, like endless stages of awakening. It seems that the more we want nirvana, the more we build an exaggerated concept around it.

So the analogy of muddy water and pure water directly deconstructs the exaggerations about nirvana, pointing out the crux of the matter. In that sense, samsara and nirvana are consciousness falling asleep and waking up. That's pretty much it. When consciousness falls asleep, we call it samsara. When consciousness wakes up, we call it nirvana. When consciousness falls asleep in the bed of unawareness, the dream of samsara appears. That is the dream we are living in right now, and it can be beautiful, like our dreams at night. Other times, the dream gets dark with nightmares, just like times we go through in life.

There are many moments during our lives when all our mental activities and the usual cognizant mind go back into alaya. This happens during deep sleep as well as when we are totally mindless, dozing off. It can even happen in deep meditative absorption. The Dzogchen masters say that there is nothing wrong with falling into alaya while you are meditating because it is not like you are just asleep. Since it happens in the context of meditation, there is merit in it. In general, then you are able to recognize that you are falling into alaya and with that recognition, you can enter awareness. That simple shift from alaya to awareness can lead you to a very powerful awakening experience. Whereas if you are not able to eventually shift from alaya to awareness, then your meditation becomes mindless, and it is thought to have very little impact on your consciousness, lacking the potency to bring about authentic awakening.

Mind-Consciousness and Great Wisdom

Another distinction is between *yid shee* (W. *yid shes*), mind-consciousness, and the great wisdom, *sherab chenpo* (W. *shes rab chen po*). *Yid shee* is one of the primary consciousnesses according to Buddhist treatises such as Abhidharma. It is often defined as a specific state of mind in these treatises. But here in this context, *yid shee* refers to our ordinary mind, including our concepts and ideas that occur in everyday life. It is an unenlightened state of our mind that perceives reality through the lens of duality. Unless we are in awareness, most of the time we are seeing everything—life, reality, events, relationships, or anything in our mind—through the lens of *yid shee*, or mind-consciousness. This is considered the samsaric mind rather than enlightened mind. It is completely lost in duality and does not see the nondual nature of all things. In other words, it doesn't see the true nature of reality as it is. Even if this samsaric mind attempts to see the nature of reality, it only gains a conceptual understanding and worldly wisdom, as it never can see the true nature of reality fully.

Great wisdom, or sherab chenpo, is not just wisdom but transcendent wisdom beyond all conceptual understanding of the nature of reality. It sees the nature of reality as it is without the slightest obscuration. When this great wisdom happens in our consciousness, it is another name for the state of consciousness that is fully awakened, freed from delusions, and sees the truth in all things. From that state, our suffering collapses.

Sentient Beings and Buddhas

The other distinctions listed in the verse are similar. Finally we come to the distinction between sentient beings and buddhas. Sentient beings are those who forgot the nature of reality and forgot who they are. They are lost in their own projections, confusions, and misconstrue the illusion of duality as reality. Through that, they are trapped in karmic chains and wander in samsara again and again. Whereas a buddha is someone who is awakened from that whole illusion and simply sees the primordial nature of reality. This distinction is pointing out that while they are different, they are not intrinsically different. They both possess buddha nature, and the sentient being is not destined to be deluded forever. A sentient being can be fully awakened to samyaksambuddhahood. In that sense, their true nature is not diametrically opposed to the nature of a buddha.

In Buddhist literature, there is a beautiful story that points out the difference as well as the sameness of buddhas and sentient beings. Two people are residing in a precious palace endowed with riches. One is sleeping and one is awake. The one who is sleeping is dreaming of hardships. The one who is awake realizes her friend is tormented in the dream but doesn't need to be, since they are in this beautiful palace. So she tries to wake up her friend. The one who is awake is the buddha and the one who is asleep is a metaphor for sentient beings. Trying to wake someone up represents the buddha's intent to lead others to liberation. The analogy is saying they are both living in the same palace, and there is no fundamental difference between them except that one is awake and realizes she is living in a beautiful palace while the other does not. The truth is that we are all living in this beautiful palace, which is the nature of reality that is forever free.

Even though the distinctions may give the sense that, for example, alaya and dharmakaya are in juxtaposition with each other, in the realm of the ultimate truth, their natures are not opposed. Their true nature is the same in the ultimate truth. So the word *expanse* in the verse refers to their true nature, or the ultimate truth. The verse is stating that while we are practicing Dzogchen, it is important to be aware of the distinctions so we won't be trapped by alaya or mind. The ultimate goal is to come to the realization that the true nature of alaya, mind, and so forth are the same as dharmakaya, wisdom, and so forth. This is taught again and again in the authoritative Dzogchen writings of the past.

Without that realization, there is a duality in which we perceive alaya as intrinsically flawed, which is not the case. What is called "the great union" is the realm of the highest truth in which the true nature of everything is the same. No duality remains; only the same taste, only one flavor, remains. That flavor is indescribable.

From the *Sharp Vajra of Awareness Tantra*, the sixth chapter on revealing clear distinctions and vital points of the practice.

VII. How to Practice the Path of Luminosity: Leaping-Over

Likewise, actualization of the nature of reality is the Great Completion.
By the wisdom that properly realizes such truth,
One should synthesize view, meditation, and conduct into one essential point.

Even within Dzogchen, there are different systems of practices all built upon the same foundation. Among them, the highest system is known as *upadesha*, the class of pith instructions. Within that, there are two systems, *trekchöd* and *tögal*, which we mentioned earlier in this book. In its etymology, *trekchöd* means cutting through dualism, and *tögal* means leaping over, which gives the impression that the process of awakening through these practices is swift and direct.

Dzogchen is also built upon the system of view, meditation, and conduct, like other systems in the Buddhist tradition. Usually view is the philosophical understanding about reality. Meditation is the practice that allows one to experience that understanding with more than just intellectual comprehension. Conduct is carrying such understanding into everyday life in order to embody it. Conduct is also a way of life that supports one's path to awakening in relationship to the first two: view and meditation.

In Dzogchen, the view is asserted as that which transcends all reference points, meditation is that which goes beyond any grasping, and conduct is that which goes beyond effort.

Since Dzogchen is nondual, in the ultimate sense it transcends any theories about reality, since all theories are either totally mistaken or a partial understanding of reality. Even the theories pointing out the ultimate truth of the nature of reality are limited. They are like a finger pointing to the moon—the finger is not the moon. A theory is like the finger trying to show you where the moon is. In that sense, Dzogchen transcends all theories. That is the view of Dzogchen. So the Dzogchen view is unlike the views or doctrines in other Buddhist traditions that hold onto a reference point as the framework of the truth. Therefore, the Dzogchen view is also unlike most other philosophical principles, which often come with something to be asserted or solidified as the perfect theory or conceptual framework that defines reality. In that sense, going beyond views is the Dzogchen view.

Dzogchen meditation is that which transcends grasping. This is in harmony with the view. Because there is no reference point in the view, there is no object in meditation that one should meditate on or hold onto as the ultimate truth. Just like the view, meditation has no reference point. It is more with letting go of all opinions and ideas about everything, and allowing oneself to abide in the nature of reality, which often is revealed by itself when the mind is no longer creating veils between oneself and the nature of reality.

Dzogchen conduct transcends effort, whereas conduct in many other systems is based on effort with respect to what is to be abandoned and what is to be cultivated. Conduct in Dzogchen is to live in awareness in all situations and not to live life guided by conceptual guidelines. Instead, it is to live and act out of awareness that is in harmony with the true nature of reality. Without trying to direct your conduct each day or each moment, your conduct will be naturally wholesome, as it is an expression of awareness rather than a result of being fooled by karmic habits and impulses.

Living the Wisdom of Dzogchen

It is important for individuals to really understand the view, meditation, and conduct of Dzogchen and fully integrate all of them with life, living without any separation between life and the wisdom of Dzogchen. In that way, all your karmic habits in your consciousness will be exhausted one after the other. There is a point when you feel you are no longer living out of ego or samsaric consciousness but that you are living out of your true nature, pure awareness. This is not an impossible feat. There are many individuals who actually arrived at a place in their life where they felt that Dzogchen was fully merged into their consciousness, and they were able to live out of that in everyday life. They experienced *guyang lobde* (W. *gu yangs blo bde*), being carefree and happy.

Religious traditions are often built upon a very important point, which is their view or doctrine about life and the mystery of existence. Whereas Dzogchen teaches that any kind of view can be confining if one is attached to it, since many of them are purely mental constructs. Remember that Dzogchen is pointing out a view that goes beyond the mind. Such a transcendent view can be brought to life through meditating on it. Once you meditate on that transcendent view and learn to live in that state throughout your day, eventually you feel that something has died inside you. What dies is the old self, the karmic imprints, pain, and suffering, and you feel that you are literally reborn into a new person even though your body is the same. This radical transformation can happen through practicing Dzogchen.

Living with Dzogchen as a part of your life is different from living life based on some doctrine. With a doctrine, there are concepts about how to live, what to do, and what not to do. The superego is still in charge as the driver in your life telling you how to act, where to go, where not to go, what to eat and not to eat, and so forth. It's all the show of the superego even if the way of life is totally wholesome. But with Dzogchen, your life is not a show of superego but just a beautiful expression of pure, egoless awareness.

**The supreme path of all paths, the shortcut,
the essential Dharma,
Endowed with the splendid wisdom-eye, direct perception,
and siddhis;
The great transference of consciousness;
The path of leaping-over: one would be swiftly liberated by
relying on it.**

Now the text introduces tögal, or leaping over, which is the last stage of Dzogchen practice. It involves working with channels and sacred visions. Yet it is said that one has to have already practiced trekchöd and had profound insight through it prior to the practice of tögal. This is logical because trekchöd is about cutting through the chain of dualism that is built upon concepts and ideas, which is the reification of reality. In some sense, the trekchöd method is very simple since it emphasizes the direct experience of the nature of reality, or awareness. There is even a famous saying that if one has not cut through the solidity of dualism through trekchöd, then the practice of tögal is like the antics of a child.

Authoritative treatises often encourage completing trekchöd practice in order to have nondual understanding before one engages with tögal practices. Otherwise some of the techniques of tögal or visions would be tainted by dualism and could even be reified, which defeats the very purpose of the practice. The practice of tögal would be purposeless without having nondual wisdom as its foundation. Once one has experienced pure awareness, rigpa, then the practice of tögal would be complementary to it and could catapult one into a whole new level of awakening.

Also, through tögal practice, one would gain various siddhis, such as profound insight and understanding about life and the world. In other words, one would gain extraordinary intuitive wisdom that can understand things which had been a mystery up to that point. This is not just a theory but happened to many individuals throughout history. There are Dzogchen yogis who are alive today who have achieved siddhis through practicing tögal and demonstrate extraordinary wisdom beyond the level of our mundane consciousness. These siddhis are witnessed by other people again and again.

For example, one of Dudjom Lingpa's disciples, a yogi named Anam Chatralwa, practiced both trekchöd and tögal in Dudjom Lingpa's lineage. This yogi was a renunciate who lived in a hermitage his entire life. He lived in a tent in the mountains, surviving on very basic Tibetan staples like barley flour, and did not intentionally gather many followers. But there were many people who held this yogi in high regard, and now and then, he allowed some people to visit him.

One time, a nomadic man visited this yogi in his hermitage. At the same time, the nomadic man's teenage children went to watch a tantric Buddhist sacred dance in another area. Remember, this took place in the early twentieth century, without cell phones. While the nomad and yogi were having a conversation, the yogi changed his facial expression and suddenly said, "Uh oh! Your kids are in trouble." He immediately started doing prayers and then said, "Now I think they are okay." Later, the nomad returned to his home, and his kids also came home. They said that at the sacred dance gathering, another group of people started a brawl with them, pulling out knives. Luckily a second group arrived and separated everyone, and no one got hurt. This all happened at the same time as the yogi had said that to their father.

There are many stories like this. Many of these stories are told by individuals who are known for integrity and honesty, and are regarded as reliable sources. It seems that sometimes these siddhis can be witnessed more in certain times and cultures. If the culture is open to it, people may witness more of these events.

Shortcut to Enlightenment

One of the main premises of Dzogchen is that one can become enlightened in a very short period of time. In that sense, the premise of Dzogchen is very radical in relation to other systems. Other tantric systems have their own process of enlightenment, which may not be as lengthy as the Sutrayana but still takes many lifetimes. Dzogchen emphasizes that enlightenment can happen in a radical manner. This is expressed in the famous Dzogchen saying that when you sit on the meditation seat, you can be deluded. By the time you get up, you could be enlightened. It says that the whole process can take just one session of meditation. This does not mean that it happens to everyone who practices Dzogchen meditation. It is very individual. There is a saying that it is not enough to practice Dzogchen, you have to *be Dzogchen*.

The idea of enlightenment in one lifetime is a fundamental principal of Anuttarayoga Tantra, which includes Dzogchen. It teaches that one can start from scratch and become enlightened, and it doesn't matter who you are—a Brahmin, an untouchable—it transcends gender, race, caste, and so forth. In today's world, it would mean that anybody can be enlightened in one lifetime, regardless of your role or your profession. You don't have to officially be a renunciant, nun, or monk. You can be a layperson, married, blue-collar worker, white-collar worker, and so forth.

So what is enlightenment? This is one of the most important questions to ask, after reading about it quite a lot in this text. The truth is there is no universal agreement on the definition, and it is defined differently even among various Buddhist doctrines. The term is not always used with the same meaning. Sometimes you can say enlightenment is buddhahood beyond human reach. Other times it is awakening or spiritual development that is accessible to us. It is important to be very open-minded toward its definition and not be very dogmatic.

Often Dzogchen and Mahamudra masters use the term *enlightenment* in a way that is accessible, which gives us the sense that it is something that we can achieve. In the simplest terms, it is about seeing the true nature of reality and not being so fettered by kleshas. You can relax about being human and having kleshas because you can be quite free inside even while the kleshas dance.

The logic behind Dzogchen as a shortcut is that enlightenment is about returning to our unconditioned nature of mind, which is already in each of us; that is, the luminous nature of mind. Dzogchen takes us there in a most direct fashion. It doesn't take us through a zigzag path to get there. As an analogy, imagine there is a destination that is nearby. You can walk there directly, which would take a short time. Or you can follow a complex map that takes you even further away away. You might get there after a long time, and the destination may not even be in your sight for a while. Whereas the system of Dzogchen is pointing out that you can see the destination—"look, it's over there"—and you can walk there in a straight fashion without any unnecessary steps. Once you get there, of course, you realize the destination was always within you.

Some say this is a perfect time for people to practice a non-religious, nondual spiritual path such as Dzogchen. There is even a prediction in ancient Buddhist writings that someday there would be a time when people would be afflicted inside with laziness toward spiritual practice yet they would be extremely intelligent. That would be the perfect time for the world to embrace Dzogchen. Some lamas say this is that time.

The first moment of consciousness arising into objects
Creates contaminated appearances. Forcefully
Transforming them into pure dharmadhatu is the
pith instruction of transference.

Now tögal instructions begin. Tögal is the most exalted practice, even more so than trekchöd, because it forcefully takes all the impure appearances created by delusion and karma and transfers them into the expanse of pristine luminosity. Here, the word *transference* has the meaning of transforming. *Forcefully* here means it is a radical method. It means not going through the usual exhausting practices; it is immediate and happens right away, whether you are ready or not to transform consciousness. It's like someone put a sacred hallucinogen in your cup and you drink it, and suddenly you are awakened. The practices of tögal are like that but of course, the intention is quite different from hallucinogens since the intention is to wake up.

The practice of tögal is very unique and it differs from other transformative practices in the Vajrayana tradition. In some sense, it applies methods but its methods are quite different from other tantric methods, which are considered contrived from the Dzogchen point of view. Tögal uses your senses as a doorway to enlightenment. One could say that it is more like a sense-based practice, rather than a mind-based practice. It does not involve too much mental reflection. Instead, it is about sitting in the right posture and using your natural senses to have meditative visions that are considered the expression of the nature of mind. These meditative visions occur within the tögal practice through the use of specific techniques and by holding the right intentions, as described in the Dzogchen teachings. Through that, enlightenment can occur and will have a very powerful impact.

In general, the very moment that our mind perceives the world, that world is simply an obscured version of the reality of the world. It is a creation of our mind that is contaminated by mental habits, delusion, and unawareness. Such a dualistic mind sees an inherent duality between perceived and perceiver, and it labels and judges what is perceived. It firmly reifies that unenlightened perception. Through the tögal practices, by generating the meditative visions, our unenlightened perception is transformed into a sacred perception. The meditative visions will also go through changes as our tögal practice progresses.

Tögal in some ways is difficult to categorize. Even though it involves working with channels, or nadis, as well as visions, it is not similar to the practice of working with channels and visions described in other Vajrayana traditions. The major difference between tögal and other Vajrayana practices is that tögal does not apply any methods that contrive the natural flow and rhythm of your consciousness and subtle body. It uses what is already there. The visions that happen in tögal are not considered manufactured visions. Rather they are considered expressions of the pure nature of your consciousness, whereas other Vajrayana practices produce visions, but they are manufactured, and not the spontaneous expression of the pure nature of your consciousness. The meditative visions of tögal are not manufactured. Instead, some of the simple techniques that the meditator uses are a catalyst to let the natural inner expression of rigpa shine outward.

Tögal does not use deliberate visualizations to create the visions. They happen on their own when one is doing the practice correctly because they are the uncontrived, natural expression of rigpa within yourself. Whereas, for example, the creation stage of Vajrayana is the opposite in its use of techniques. It involves the meditator deliberately using visualizations to create images like mandalas and deities in his or her mind.

Many Vajrayana methods often involve manipulating one's mind and subtle body, and as a result, a variety of visions can emerge as a sign of progress. It's not that those signs are not meaningful; they are signs that a powerful awakening is happening in one's consciousness. Yet the signs are considered contrived because our mind manufactured them rather than their being a natural expression of our original awareness that resides in each of us from time immemorial. So Vajrayana visions differ from tögal visions in that the Vajrayana visions are artificial. An analogy for tögal visions is that they are like the natural light shining through the window versus the artificial light from a sun lamp.

The Category of Lamps

All the tögal practices generally revolve around fundamental principles such as the *drön ma* (W. *sgron ma*), or lamps. Those who want to practice tögal need to understand the lamps not just intellectually but with first-hand knowledge of them by practicing tögal and recognizing each of the lamps through one's own direct experience.

The well-known categories of four or five lamps as well as six lamps are not always the same in the Dzogchen texts, although there is no contradiction between them; their essential meaning is the same in all the versions. We will describe the relevant ones here.

In order to practice tögal, we need to know how the lamps work with each other. They all work in conjunction with each other so that the tögal visions and stages of awakening can take place. This will also lead us to understand our physical and subtle bodies in general. Some of the lamps describe visions that occur in one's meditation and some describe channels in our body. Some of them describe neither visions nor subtle channels but the experience of awakening to the nature of mind.

In our physical body, the heart area is called the *citta flesh lamp*. A thin channel goes through the middle of our body, similar to the idea of the central channel, but Dzogchen asserts this is slightly different from the *avadhuti* or central channel in other systems. It is known as *kati,* hollow inside, also called the *lamp of white, soft, hollow, crystal channel.*

In the retina of each eye, there are two subtle channels that emerge from that central channel. These two subtle channels together are called the *water-lamp of the far-reaching lasso*. In general, our eyes see ordinary forms in the world, but these particular channels are capable of seeing sacred visions as an expression of the nature of our consciousness. The channels are not made out of ordinary karmic factors; some dimension of them is considered what is called a *light-channel,* which is not an ordinary channel, due to its ability to capture sacred visions.

A little clarification: sometimes people might interpret this particular lamp as just the eye, but it is more than that. The main etymology of *water-lamp of the far-reaching lasso* relates to how your mind is lassoed, or bound: when you see forms outside, if you don't realize that all the ordinary forms that the eye is witnessing are simply a display of your own mind, you are catapulted far away into samsara, which binds (lassos) your awareness. If you realize the forms as a display, you are catapulted into nirvana, and this binds your mind from wandering into delusion. It also means that you can see far away. It is called *water-lamp* because it serves as a medium through which the mind is moistened by the bliss of samadhi, the non-grasping at appearances. It is called *lamp* because it allows the sacred visions to increase in your experience.

Posture and Sight

Once you are ready to practice tögal, the ideal place and time is where there are not many activities to distract you, a little bit further away from civilization, during a season when the sky is usually clear. Obviously, the seasons when the sky is generally clear is related to geography. For example, in Tibet, autumn is a great time to do tögal practice.

There are also specific postures known as the dharmakaya posture of a lion, the sambhogakaya posture of a reclining elephant, and the nirmanakaya posture of a sage. It is best not to get hung up on the details of the postures but rather just be in the right state of mind or openness so the experiences can arise.

It is recommended to not engage with any kind of speech, not even reciting mantras or sutras. Leave all activities behind, spiritual or sacred, and don't do anything, while breathing naturally without any special techniques. Don't even meditate and don't engage with visualizations from Vajrayana, such as constructing mandalas or forms of deities. Just leave your mind as it is and don't get attached to any of your experiences, thoughts, feelings, and so on. Don't try to make anything happen deliberately. Just wait and see what naturally appears to your consciousness. It would be essential in this practice to intuitively feel that you are in touch with your subtle channels. Then the sacred visions can open.

There are also simple techniques using sight. For example, you can direct your gaze about an arm-length away toward the sun with eyes half-open. It is sometimes recommended that beginners look toward the west in the morning and toward the east in the evening. You can also look at the moon in a similar manner.

Visions Emerge

Eventually visions will arise one after the other. First, a blue radiance like the color of the sky appears in the space in front of you, resembling the sky itself. Then the five colors emerge, unfurling like silk brocade. This is known as *the lamp of the pristine space*. Remember that the space you are witnessing is not outside but a direct reflection of your own pure awareness that resides within you. In that same space also arises the *lamp of empty bindus*, which are five-colored circles, often compared to the concentric patterns created on small pond by throwing a rock into it.

Sitting in the postures and gazing in the manner we described above, directly looking without any effort, allow yourself to merge into those colors without distraction or any other activity. Soon, pristine, nondual awareness is revealed by itself. Often this will manifest in profound insights or understanding about the nature of reality, as if a sea of wisdom erupted from within. This is known as the *self-occurring wisdom lamp.*

Following that experience, a vision emerges called the *vajra-strand*, which resembles a strand of pearls or golden thread. When it arises, bring that strand into the *bindus* or circles of lights in the space you are witnessing. The shape will eventually change into a lace-like shape. Again, do not analyze the visions, neither reifying them nor getting attached to them.

All these are common instructions in early Dzogchen literature including the Dzogchen Tantras and writings of well-known Dzogchen masters. Traditionally, practitioners are not supposed to do these practices on their own unless they have received oral teachings from a Dzogchen master. Sometimes there are preparatory practices before a practitioner is allowed to begin this practice. With proper instructions from a skilled Dzogchen master, these practices are proven to be very powerful. Many yogis in Tibet experienced profound awakening from the tögal practices.

The first consciousness arising as the appearance of clear light
Will become a spectacle for the wisdom-eye.
Appearances will arise and increase as the great luminosity.
Awareness will ripen as essence, and manifest and display as mudras.
The expansive nature of reality, where appearances and experiences are exhausted, will be reached.

In tögal, just as in any other system, there are stages of meditative experiences, which are known as the four visions; in Tibetan, *nang wa zhi* (W. *snang ba bzhi*). They are: direct perception of the nature of reality, increasing of meditative experience, maturation of awareness, and dissolution of visions. These experiences can occur to those who are trained in Vajrayana, such as those who have gone through *ngondro* (W. *sngon 'gro*), preliminary practices, because their consciousness is imbued with the Tantric Buddhist icons, archetypes, and forms. For this reason, tögal is not meant to be done just by reading a book but by going through the training under the direction of a skilled master.

The first vision is the stage of directly witnessing or perceiving the display of the luminous nature of mind. At this stage, the very moment the mind engages with its own field of perception, it is no longer deluded, and it is free from the veils of erroneous perceptions. It sees the way things are. As the direct realization of the true nature of reality arises, a variety of visions also appear as a natural expression of rigpa, such as a blue radiance pervading space, circles of lights, bindus, and so forth. These were described in the previous section. Traditional texts lay out the particular signs of this stage that a meditator may experience, such as losing any desire to be active, move around, or utter ordinary speech.

Your mind becomes flexible, and you feel you can direct your mind anywhere you want.

The second vision is the increasing of meditative experience. The experience of awakening to the true nature of reality is becoming more mature and stabilized in one's consciousness. It is accompanied by signs such as seeing bright visions of the five colors or seeing forms resembling stupas, lotuses, lattices, and so forth. The meditator may have unpredictable experiences such as sickness, discomfort, or losing inhibitions and wanting to move or sing spiritual songs spontaneously. The meditator's mind has no internal restraint.

The third vision is maturation of awareness. In that stage, the awakening experience becomes matured and fully integrated with one's consciousness. It is said that signs of this stage may appear in the form of palaces, mandalas, images of the five buddha families, heruka families, five bindus, and so forth. Internally, one experiences gaining mastery of one's mind and prana.

The last stage is the dissolution of everything into *dharmata*, absolute reality. In that moment, all the sacred visions that the meditator is experiencing dissolves. The whole point of the practice of tögal is to have the sacred visions and ultimately dissolve them. This is when one's consciousness becomes enlightened.

These experiences and forms will be natural and have profound significance for yogis and meditators who are trained in Tantric Buddhism because, as we said, their consciousness is familiar with Tantric Buddhist philosophies, archetypes, and icons. That being said, someone who is not trained in Tantric Buddhism might have different experiences on their own journey to awakening. Even though these forms and signs will be different for each individual, the idea of enlightenment is the same, which is to be free from all our delusions, to see the true nature of reality, and to fully embody that awakening.

One will be awakened into the great transference,
the youthful vase body.
As a sign, it would be like space dissolves into space,
Beyond lifespan, time periods, and limitations.

It is said that once one reaches the advanced stage of tögal practice, then complete enlightenment, which is called "the great transference of the youthful vase body," can be actualized in a very short period of time. (The youthful vase body is described in more detail in the next chapter.)

Sometimes traditional texts give a precise time frame for achieving complete enlightenment. This is quite standard in many Buddhist traditions. For example, in the Theravadin tradition, one of the most revered texts is the *Satipatthana Sutra*, which lays out the four foundations of mindfulness. At the end of the sutra, it describes how long it would take for someone to achieve enlightenment. It goes from seven years to seven months and finally to seven days. Dzogchen states that one can achieve complete enlightenment, the great transference, through tögal practice, either in ten days, five months, or ten months. Yet one should keep in mind that enlightenment described in the *Satipatthana Sutra* and tögal are not the same because of their different doctrines.

Giving a time frame to the process of enlightenment is a very uplifting narrative, especially when the time is not too long. Perhaps one of the reasons very specific numbers are mentioned in the Dzogchen tradition is because Dzogchen says that enlightenment can happen at any given moment. Yet it has different time frames because the process of enlightenment is completely dependent on the individual. Two people might practice the same system but may not progress at the same speed. The inner process can have different speeds due to many factors from inside as well as outside; that is, not just whether one's consciousness is ready to be free but also external factors such as the master you are studying with and even the people you are hanging out with. If you are studying with an extraordinary master, such as H. H. Jigme Phuntsok, and you are surrounded by very evolved Dzogchen yogis, that auspicious environment will help expedite your journey to enlightenment. So the shortened time period for the journey to enlightenment is welcome news. It enables us to have the aspiration to be awakened in this very lifetime, in this very body.

Once one becomes fully enlightened, one goes "beyond lifespans" and time frames, which are limitations that only exist in the realm of the conditioned, or samsara. Those limitations are transcended in the realm of nirvana, or the absolute truth. Let's clarify: This does not mean that once you become fully awakened through tögal practice, you will not die and you will live forever. That's not what *beyond lifespans* means. It means that your consciousness is free from any kind of dualistic reference point, and you don't feel bound to all the earthly conditions.

Three types of liberation into the pure rainbow body
will occur.
Because of various indefinite experiences,
Happiness and suffering will occur again and again.
One should take all of them into dharmadhatu
without hope and fear.

The Dzogchen tradition lays out a system of enlightenment and its impact, including signs of enlightenment. Other Buddhist systems, such as Vajrayana and Sutrayana, do this as well. In Dzogchen, there is an attainment called "liberation into the rainbow body," which comes with three different signs that occur at the time of death. These signs are considered indications that the individual is enlightened, in the context of tögal practice. The details of these signs are mentioned in various Tibetan commentaries on this tantra with slightly different interpretations between each of them.

One kind of rainbow body is that one's body dissolves completely without any remnants, the way a rainbow dissolves into the sky. Another type of rainbow body at the time of death is that one's body is surrounded by rainbows for a few days, and then eventually dissolves without any remnants. Another type of rainbow body is that the body begins to slowly shrink and eventually dissolves into rainbow light within seven days, only leaving behind hair and nails.

Even though these three miraculous signs are taught in the Dzogchen system, miraculous signs of awakening are also mentioned in all Buddhist systems. For example, when someone becomes an arhat, it is said there are also external signs. The Pali sutras state that when Siddhartha became enlightened, the earth shook. There are different ways of interpreting these miracles based on one's understanding.

The heart of the matter is that when one is enlightened, one's consciousness is completely freed from all types of karmic patterns, and there is no longer a basis in one's consciousness where karmic patterns can be stored. The meaning behind all the miraculous signs is that one's consciousness is fully enlightened, and the signs are just an expression of that.

Transient Meditative Experiences

During the tögal practices, there will be a variety of *nyams*, or meditative experiences. They are often transient and can be very colorful. You might feel hypersensitive, and the experiences can be extreme in either way—good or bad. For example, you could have unbearable joy in one moment, and in the next moment, that could change. A multitude of visions could occur to the meditator that are unusual and not part of normal daily life. The practitioner must stay grounded in the nondual view, not get attached to any of the experiences or visions, and see that they are all a display of their own consciousness.

Even the sacred mandalas and buddhas in the visions are not coming from outside. In general, visions in other traditions are attributed to an external, supernatural force. They might not be seen as a display of your own consciousness but rather as if some divine entity has appeared to you, just like seeing someone when you run into people on the street in daily life. Often there is a duality between oneself and the visions.

These verses are encouraging us to remember that whenever visions arise, they are not as they appear. Even when buddhas appear, they are not enlightened beings popping up from somewhere else with a consciousness separate from yours. Instead, remember that they are a display of your own pure consciousness, the dharmakaya mind. Remain in the place where there is nothing to reject and nothing to grasp. Then there is a doorway to liberation in each of the experiences.

Those who have not completed the path in such a way
Should understand the vital point of view and meditation like a swallow entering its nest.
Recognize the bardo of dying as a beautiful woman looks at her own reflection.
Recognize the nature of reality like meeting with a familiar person.
Enter into the expanse of luminosity like a child jumping into its mother's lap.
Continue the pith instructions like installing a pipe to channel water.
Block the entrance to samsara, like a criminal released from prison.
It is essential to have the vital points of these six analogies.
By such means, it is possible that one will be liberated or relieved.

Those who have not reached complete enlightenment, who still have karmic patterns in their consciousness to be purified, can engage with Dzogchen practice and find an opening where they can experience total liberation. This brings up the topic of the bardo. *Bardo* means "between state," even though all the times and periods of our life are illusions. In the realm of the true nature of reality, there is no time and no period between birth and death. Yet in the realm of relative truth, there is everything—birth, death, and successive stages of individual life that each of us can experience. As an analogy, if you imagine your life is like a year, then the bardos would be like different seasons. Yet they are all part of the same cycle of a year. There are different ways of categorizing the bardos, such as the four bardos—the bardo of birth, bardo of dying, bardo of dharmata, and bardo of becoming.

Bardo of Birth

The first bardo is the period from the moment we are born to the moment of our death; in other words, our life. It is already happening right now in this very moment to each of us. From the moment we are born from our mother's womb, everything we go through as a human being until we meet death is encompassed by the bardo of birth. It comes with a lot of sorrow as well as so much joy.

This bardo is more than being stuck in this life doing ordinary things and being just another human locked up in collective habits, lost in our egos, playing a competitive survival game, and trying to gain security, achievements, and happiness. If we live like that, life is like a dead end. Whereas this bardo could be turned into a wonderful spiritual season where we cultivate reflection and practice the Dharma. We would be moving toward awakening while living life on earth along with everyone else.

The way to find liberation in this bardo is through embracing the Dharma and an enlightened view that can free us from our mistaken perception of reality. Meditation can unburden our consciousness from the weight of all the kleshas.

Here, this verse is encouraging us to immerse ourself into the ultimate Dharma, the path of Dzogchen. The image of a swallow entering its nest is a very popular analogy in Dzogchen writings to depict immersing oneself into something without any hesitation or resistance.

Bardo of Dying

The bardo of dying is when we go through the different stages of dying known as the dissolutions. These are often mentioned in the tantric treatises. This is also a moment when one can remember to meditate and reside in the nondual view of Dzogchen. Sometimes other people, such as a spiritual master, can offer oral guidance to lead the dying person into a meditative state so the person can experience the luminous nature of consciousness and be enlightened on the spot. The analogy of a beautiful person looking in the mirror is an image of recognizing the luminous nature of mind.

It is said that the second bardo is a period where everyone has a chance to glimpse the nature of consciousness. But if someone has no meditation practice, they would not recognize it. If someone has the capacity to recognize the pure nature of consciousness arising in that process, he or she could be liberated in that moment.

Bardo of Dharmata

The third bardo is the bardo of dharmata, which appears after one dies. Then one's whole reality becomes a journey of consciousness. During the bardo of dharmata, there is also an opportunity to recognize the luminous nature of your own mind, as if you are meeting with someone you know, like meeting with an old friend. This is also the bardo where archetypal visions arise, such as herukas, specific *ishtadevatas,* or wrathful and peaceful deities. Of course, those visions are from the spiritual path that one has walked in their lifetime.

During the appearances of these forms, you recognize them not as coming from outside but as the display of your own mind. You recognize that the very source of the visions is intrinsic to your consciousness. They are already there as a potential and now they emerge. But this is all happening in your consciousness—they arise from your consciousness and happen in your consciousness.

If you remember there is no duality between yourself and these forms, you would be liberated in that very moment. Your consciousness would return to the womb of the primordial ground, the original luminosity. This is explained with the analogy of a child returning to the lap of its mother.

Bardo of Becoming

During the bardo of becoming, which is a period of taking a new rebirth, there is still an open opportunity where one can be awakened or freed. The key point is to realize what is happening in that very moment. It is a time for one to use the Vajrayana trainings from this life and visualize that one is moving toward the buddha realms. That practice is exemplified by the analogy of using a pipe to channel water.

Then one can intentionally block the doorway to samsara and be liberated in the buddha realms. Buddha realms are not outside of one's consciousness but are states of consciousness that are already free and enlightened. The analogy for such liberation is of a prisoner escaping from jail forever.

The Liberating Power of Bardo Teachings

These teachings on the bardo are about finding liberation in the four bardos according to the Dzogchen system. In the Nyingma tradition, people often study and engage with mental exercises to develop readiness to face the bardos and to train one's mind to stay in awareness all the time, whether one is alive, dying, or traveling in a bardo realm. It is an important part of the Dzogchen training.

Because there are numerous books written on the bardo available in many languages, the word *bardo* has become almost a household word, appearing even in popular songs and on common signs. While reading books about the bardo can be intellectually entertaining, you would not get the full benefit of the bardo teachings. The bardo teachings should not become an intellectual fetish or entertainment. The transforming power of the bardo teachings comes through practicing them with visualizations and reflections.

In Tibet, there is a tradition of people spending time in intensive retreats simulating the process of going through the bardos, bringing to consciousness the possibility of one's own death. One can overcome fears and learn to recognize visions and projections as purely the display of one's own mind and not externalize them.

This process is more than preparing for bardos in the future. In such an intensive retreat, you are able to be in touch with the luminous nature of your mind. You learn to recognize your own projections, which will run your life until such insight happens. You can leave such a retreat with a feeling that you are ready to live and you are ready to die. You will feel that there is nothing to fear.

That is the liberation you can experience in the realm of now. Then you can live in that liberation regardless of what befalls you.

From the *Sharp Vajra of Awareness Tantra*, the seventh chapter on how to practice the path of the luminosity: leaping-over.

VIII. Revealing The Way Ground Abides

Ultimately, the result of complete liberation
Is the dharmakaya of the ground, buddha nature,
Spontaneously present as the dharmakaya Primordial Lord.
The object of attainment is the youthful vase body.

All Mahayana Buddhist traditions have various terms for spiritual attainment. The name for the highest attainment often includes the word *kaya,* such as the dimension of enlightened mind called dharmakaya as well as "the youthful vase body." The Sanskrit word *kaya* means body, but *body* should not be conflated with the usual meaning of the word as a concrete object. Those who are not familiar with this term or have not studied Mahayana and Vajrayana can sometimes mistakenly think that kaya always has to do with a physical entity.

There is a humorous and true anecdote about how *youthful vase body* can be mistakenly construed as the physical body of an enlightened person. Once, an American Buddhist student finished a traditional three-year retreat during which he chanted many sadhanas and read many liturgies filled with Tibetan Buddhist terminology. He was moved by his teacher's guidance and felt incredible devotion toward his lama during the closing ceremony, so he wrote a traditional-style hymn to express his deep feelings. Traditionally, Tibetan Buddhist poetic similes are used for the mind, speech, and body of an enlightened being, such as "Your speech is as pleasant as the music of a gandharva, your mind is as deep as the ocean," and so forth. The student used these similes and then when he praised the body of his teacher, he wrote with sincerity, "Your body is the youthful vase body." His lama read it and started cracking up, saying jokingly, "Are you insinuating that I have a big belly." The student had thought that the youthful vase body was a physical body of the Buddha.

There are many humorous anecdotes about people making innocent mistakes with the best intention, misunderstanding these terms. Here, it would be worthwhile to pause and reflect on the meaning of these two terms, *dharmakaya* and *youthful vase body*. From the Dzogchen point of view, they are not different from each other. The latter is mainly used in the Dzogchen tradition and not in other tantric systems.

The Model of Three Kayas

Dharmakaya is one of the three kayas, along with sambhogakaya and nirmanakaya. The point of having the model of the three kayas is a way for our mind to capture the fullness of enlightenment—that it is not only a totally liberated state but it also has the capacity to manifest altruism and compassion in the world, and to be of help to others. If one of the three kayas is left out, then there is a theoretical glitch that would make enlightenment incomplete—either too dualistic or too dead.

For example, if there is no nirmanakaya, we would not be able to describe enlightenment as being alive; as something that moves us not to be lost in some kind of eternal peace but to actually feel compassion toward the world; not to hibernate in a cradle of eternal bliss but to connect with and be active in the world; not to just live with an egoic mind and self-centeredness but to help everyone alleviate their sorrow and find ultimate liberation. That understanding of enlightenment is very inspiring.

On the other hand, if dharmakaya is left out and there is nirmanakaya alone, then complete enlightenment becomes very concrete and dualistic, and it would not be rooted in the unconditioned.

Sambhogakaya is the bridge that connects dharmakaya and nirmanakaya. It is the unfathomable joy that comes into one's mind when one is fully enlightened. One begins to experience the sublime states of consciousness that make enlightenment feel alive. Without that experience, there is a danger that enlightenment becomes a nihilistic end of everything—end of suffering, end of self, end of samsara—without anything positive. But this is not what life is all about.

Imagine in your mind what enlightenment might be. Perhaps you have preconceived notions of it—which tends to be the case —and think that when you become enlightened, eventually you become nothing. Life just continues from there on, and you will never return to the world again. Imagine you are meditating on the cushion and feel very deep peace. All your thoughts are gone, and you imagine that you are never going to get up from the cushion from then on. You are never going to see your loved ones, you are never going to eat chocolate or listen to good music or walk in the park. It would be like that. Yes, enlightenment is the absence of delusions but it should not be the end of life or consciousness.

Dharmakaya in Dzogchen

Dharmakaya is defined slightly differently in Dzogchen compared to the general Buddhist doctrine even though the principle is the same. The usual way of interpreting dharmakaya in Buddhist systems such as Prajnaparamita treatises is intellectually complex and can sometimes be very heavy. Instead of helping you understand dharmakaya, it can defeat the purpose and create confusion. In Dzogchen texts, the way they describe dharmakaya is not so wordy and can give you a direct flavor of it in language that is more intuitive and poetic.

Dzogchen teaches that dharmakaya is not something to be obtained but already resides in the basic realm of our consciousness. This is definitely a nondual way of interpreting dharmakaya. In some ways, it is also very understandable to many people in the modern world. Not only that, often Dzogchen masters will give pointing-out instructions, *ngotrod* (W. *ngo sprod*), in which they invite you to recognize the three kayas right on the spot, not anywhere else but within your consciousness.

Dharmakaya is the source of the two other kayas as well as the source of all our experiences in the deepest sense. It is usually described as unborn, unconditioned, uncompounded, empty, without characteristics, beyond coming and going, beyond meeting and separation. It is a state of our consciousness where the thinking mind is completely dropped. What remains is what is called the luminous nature of mind, which is the dharmakaya. Not only is it the source from which all our experiences emerge, it is also the very womb into which they eventually dissolve.

Youthful Vase Body

The youthful vase body, in Tibetan, *zhön nu bum ku* (W. *gzhon nu bum sku*), is one of the most intriguing notions, and is found mainly in the Dzogchen Tantras. It is a metaphor that points out dharmakaya, buddha nature, the ground of all, the nature of consciousness, and so forth. So the definition should not be too precise, otherwise it would become a "thing" that loses its true meaning.

The youthful vase body is the dharmakaya of the ground, which is always there. But when we say "always there," please do not think in terms of time. It means it is the ground of everything, the true nature of reality. The youthful vase body is an image of a lamp burning inside a vase. The lamp symbolizes the original mind, the dharmakaya of the ground. Dzogchen says that the prana, or life force, moves and breaks that vase. Then the display of the ground-dharmakaya shines out. The whole reality manifests. If consciousness recognizes that the whole phenomenal display is none other that its own show, its own manifestation, then consciousness becomes enlightened and doesn't get lost in the trap of duality. It realizes there is no separation between self and other.

Poetically speaking, consciousness can return to the youthful vase body where there are no delusions. We don't mean physically return. It is a poetic way to say consciousness does not get lost but goes back to the place where there is no delusion in the first place.

In Dzogchen, that is the ultimate liberation—attaining the state of dharmakaya. Even though dharmakaya can never be attained, since it is already there, this seemingly paradoxical phrase is the only way to describe this nondual topic. This experience of returning to the youthful vase body or some fundamental consciousness prior to ego development can happen at any given moment. It often happens to many people during their meditation or during the practice of tantric sadhanas. It also happens during the bardo as well. Some systems teach that the bardo is a potent time where one can experience returning to the youthful vase body.

Those with the highest faculty will actualize it in one lifetime.
The middle and least ones will attain the glory of the kayas and qualities
And will be liberated in the ground of the five pure buddha realms.

Dzogchen often emphasizes becoming enlightened in this very lifetime. It is almost the premise of the tradition. Yet the level of attainment is not always the same at the individual level because everyone is very different due to internal and external conditions and circumstances that impact our consciousness. In a simple way, we could say it has a lot to do with one's own karma.

But here it says that the ones with the highest faculty, whose consciousness is ripened and ready to practice Dzogchen, will attain enlightenment in this very lifetime. This is not about just having some temporary enlightenment experience but rather that enlightenment is stabilized and integrated with one's consciousness, so one lives it.

Those who may not have the highest faculty to become fully enlightened in this lifetime will have the opportunity to become enlightened during one of the bardos, such as the bardo of dharmata. Even the ones who have the least faculty can become enlightened and return to the five buddha realms during the bardo of becoming. These buddha realms are another name for the five wisdoms (described in an earlier chapter), which are different attributes of enlightened, dharmakaya mind.

Always appearing as lords for the benefit of those to be tamed,
[They are] like a moon reflecting its image in the water.
Until samsara, the radiance, dissolves into space,
The wisdom display of space will not cease.

Becoming enlightened is a completion but not an ending. This is what these verses are continuously indicating. Samsara, the world of suffering, is a state of our mind that doesn't exist anywhere outside of ourself. There is no samsara that we can abandon, renounce, relinquish, or run away from. It is purely a state of mind and is none other than the radiance of pure consciousness whose true nature is already enlightened as the dharmakaya mind.

When consciousness becomes fully enlightened and returns to its original state, consciousness doesn't go into an eternal hibernation of ultimate peace. Consciousness continues as an amazing momentum of enlightened mind, which becomes a source of all goodness and benevolence.

In simple language, the verse is saying that once you become enlightened, you won't become some kind of happy vegetable. Instead, you fully embrace life, the world, and your relationship to everyone. You will be a source of light and love for everyone while you are truly grounded in the luminous nature of your mind. You have the ability to live in the world but not be caught up in the chains of the world. The world, regardless of being perfect or imperfect, is no longer samsara and becomes a buddha realm to you. You are the primordial lord of that realm because you have been the buddha all along.

From the *Sharp Vajra of Awareness Tantra*, the eighth chapter on revealing the way ground abides.

This work was begun on the 118th parinirvana of Dudjom Lingpa, whose words are the wisdom that dispels the darkness in the mindstream of many beings. Even though he entered parinirvana, his Dharma eye will never close; the illumination of his awakened mind will continue to shine. In doing this work, we become the harbinger of the enlightened master and serve as a vehicle to continuously let the wisdom of Dudjom Lingpa shine in the mind of countless beings in the future.

Tibetan Text and English Translation

The Sharp Vajra of Awareness Tantra

TIBETAN

དག་སྣང་ཡེ་ཤེས་དྭ་བ་ལས༔
ཀ་དག་ཀུན་ཏུ་བཟང་མོའི་དབྱིངས༔
ལྷུན་གྲུབ་རྫོགས་པ་ཆེན་པོའི་མཛོད༔
ཤེས་རིག་རྡོ་རྗེ་རྣོན་པོའི་རྒྱུད༔
གསང་ཆེན་སྦུགས་ཀྱི་ཡང་བཅུད་བཞུགས༔

རིགས་དང་དཀྱིལ་འཁོར་ཀུན་གྱི་བདག་པོ་མཆོག༔
བདེ་གཤེགས་སྙིང་པོར་མི་ཕྱེད་དད་པས་འདུད༔

I.

འཁོར་འདས་ལམ་གསུམ་མཉམ་པ་ཉིད་ཀྱི་ངང༔
སྟོང་ཁྱབ་ནམ་མཁའ་རྣམ་པར་དག་པ་རུ༔
སྤྲོས་བྲལ་ཆོས་སྐུའི་རྣལ་འབྱོར་ཆེན་པོ་ངས༔
ཡེ་ཤེས་སྒྱུ་འཕྲུལ་རྩལ་དུ་ཤར་བའི་ཚུལ༔
གཞི་ཡི་ཆོས་སྐུ་བདེ་གཤེགས་སྙིང་པོ་ཉིད༔
སྤྲོས་བྲལ་རྣམ་ཐར་གསུམ་ལྡན་ཡེ་སངས་རྒྱས༔
ལྷུན་གྲུབ་རོལ་པ་སྐུ་གསུམ་མཉམ་སྦྱོར་དབྱིངས༔
སྟོན་འཁོར་དགོངས་པ་དབྱེར་མེད་རོལ་པ་རུ༔
བདག་དང་སྐལ་བ་མཉམ་པའི་སྐྱེས་བུ་འགའི༔
ལས་སྨོན་བསོད་ནམས་བཟང་པོའི་དཔལ་དུ་ཤར༔
ལམ་འདིར་ལས་འཕྲོ་མེད་པའི་སྐྱེས་བུ་ཡིས༔
རི་མོའི་ཟས་ནོར་བཞིན་དུ་ཐོབ་ལེན་མེད༔
སྐལ་བཟང་སྐྱེས་བུ་དག་གི་སྤྱོད་ཡུལ་ལོ༔
ཆོས་ཉིད་ནམ་མཁའ་མཛོད་འདི་ཕ་ཡོག་ཕེབས༔

TRANSLATION

From the wisdom web of sacred vision,
The original purity, the expanse of Samantabhadri,
Spontaneous presence, the treasury of the Great Completion,
The Sharp Vajra of Awareness Tantra,
The quintessence of the Great Secret Mantra.

To the supreme Lord of all enlightened families and mandalas,
Buddha nature, I pay homage with undying devotion.

I. Taking the Impure Mind as the Path

Within the equality of the three: samsara, nirvana, and the path,
Empty, all-pervasive, pure space,
I, the great dharmakaya yogi, freed from the extremes,
Will illuminate how the magical display of wisdom appears as potential energy:

The ground dharmakaya, buddha nature,
Freed from the extremes, endowed with the three liberations, is primordially enlightened.

In the expanse of the union of the three kayas, the display of spontaneous presence,
The display of the inseparability of disciple and master,
Appears to myself and those who are equally fortunate
As the glory of our excellent karma, aspiration, and merit.
For individuals who do not have the fortunate karmic propensity,
There is nothing to gain or obtain on this path, just like paintings of food.
This is the domain of the fortunate individuals.
This sky-treasury of dharmata is their sublime father's legacy.

སྟོན་མཆོག་ཀུན་བཟང་ཁྱབ་བདག་རྡོ་རྗེ་ཡིས༔
སྤྲུལ་འཕྲུལ་རོལ་བའི་འཁོར་དུ་རྩོམ་པ་ལ༔
ཉོན་ཅིག་གཉིས་མེད་རོལ་པའི་རང་རྩལ་འཁོར༔

ཀུན་བྱེད་རྒྱལ་པོ་སྒོ་གསུམ་གཙོ་ལ་བརྟགས༔
ངོས་བཟུང་ཀུན་བྱེད་རྒྱལ་པོའི་གཟུགས་ཁ་དོག༔
བྱུང་གནས་འགྲོ་གསུམ་ཡུལ་མེད་ཟང་ཐལ་ངང༔
ཁྲིགས་ཆོད་ལམ་གྱི་ངོ་བོར་ལྷུན་གྱིས་གྲུབ༔

གཅིག་ཆར་གཞི་མེད་རྩ་བྲལ་ལམ་དུ་ཚུད༔
གཞན་དག་ནམ་མཁའ་དག་ལ་བབས་ཀྱིས་བཞག༔
བདུན་ཕྲག་གསུམ་གྱིས་ངེས་གསང་ལམ་དུ་འཛུད༔
དབང་པོ་དམན་པའི་རིགས་ཅན་དག་ལས་ཡང༔
གནས་དང་འགྱུ་བ་གཉིས་སུ་ངོ་སྤྲོད་ནས༔
སེམས་ལ་ལམ་བྱས་རིག་པའི་དབྱིངས་སུ་བསྐྱལ༔

དང་པོ་གཉིས་ནས་གཅིག་གྱུར་རྩེ་གཅིག་དང༔
མ་བཅོས་བཞག་པ་རང་རྩལ་མངོན་གྱུར་དང༔
སྟོང་པ་ཏར་སང་དྲན་སྟོང་ཡན་པ་དང༔
སྟོང་གསལ་དང་གནས་རང་གསལ་དྲན་པ་ཞེས༔
སྤྲོ་མ་གཉིས་ཀྱིས་གང་ཤར་མངོན་དུ་བྱེད༔
ཕྲེ་མ་གཉིས་ནི་འཛིན་སྣང་ཀོན་ལས༔
རྣམ་པར་རྟོག་པ་འགགས་པའི་མི་རྟོག་པ༔

The supreme master, Samantabhadra, universal sovereign vajra,
Manifests the miraculous display of disciples.
Listen, disciples, nondual potential energy of awareness itself:

Analyze the chief of the three gates [body, speech, and mind]—
the all-creating king.
Recognize the form and color of the all-creating king.
Analyze its origin, residence, and destination to find that it has
no place and is transparent.
This is spontaneously present in the true nature of the
path of cutting through.

One could instantaneously enter the path of no-ground and no-root.
Otherwise, they rest naturally within the pure space [of the mind].
They will enter the path of the ultimate secret within three weeks.
For those with lesser capacity,
Point out the two states of stillness and movement.
Taking the mind as the path leads to the expanse of awareness.

First, single-pointed mind on the two as one.
Then, resting without looking, the potential energy of mind itself
manifests.
Empty, suddenly wakeful, all thoughts remain empty
and unrestrained.
Remaining in empty clarity is called self-illuminated mindfulness.
The first two actualize whatever arises.
The latter two, through their mode of apprehension,
Remain in no-thought, where all mental activity has ceased.

ཀུན་ལ་བདེ་དང་སྟོང་པ་གསལ་སྣང་ཚོགས༔
ཞེན་དང་ཆགས་པའི་ཡུལ་དུ་གྱུར་པ་དང༔
ལུས་ངག་ཡིད་ལ་ན་ཚ་མི་བདེའི་ཉམས༔
སོ་ཟིན་མེད་པར་རིམ་པ་བཞིན་དུ་འབྱུང༔
བཟང་པོར་རེ་རློམས་མངོན་ཞེན་སྐྱེས་པ་དང༔
ངན་པར་དོགས་དང་གནོད་བྱེད་རང་རྒྱུད་སར༔
བལྟས་ཚད་གོལ་ཤོར་ནོར་བའི་འཕྲང་ལ་ཐོགས༔

ཀུན་གྱི་སྐྱི་ཆིངས་ལམ་གྱི་གནད་གཅིག་སྟུ༔
བདེ་སྡུག་བར་གསུམ་སྤྱོད་ཚོར་ཐམས་ཅད་ཀུན༔
བདེན་མེད་ཉམས་ཀྱི་རྫུན་རིས་ངེས་པ་རུ༔
ཤེས་ཏེ་དགག་སྒྲུབ་མེད་པར་བཞག་པས་ན༔
གོལ་ཤོར་ཚར་གཅོད་ཤེས་རབ་མིག་གཅིག་ཡིན༔

འགའ་ཞིག་བཤེས་གཉེན་དམ་པར་རིང་གྱུར་ན༔
ས་བཅད་ལྔ་པོ་ལམ་གྱི་དམ་པར་བཟུང༔
རྩེ་གཅིག་ཉམས་སུ་ལེན་ལ་བརྩོན་དྲག་ན༔
སེམས་ཀྱི་རྒྱལ་ཉམས་དྲན་པའི་ངང་བརྟན་ནས༔
མི་ཡི་ལུས་ལ་དུད་འགྲོའི་སེམས་སུ་འགྱུར༔
འགའ་ཞིག་སྒྲོ་འདོག་དག་ཏུ་འཕྱན་པར་འགྱུར༔
དེ་ཕྱིར་དགེ་བའི་བཤེས་གཉེན་འབྲལ་མེད་བསྟེན༔

All will have bliss, emptiness, and a variety of vivid appearances,
Which all can become objects of attachment and grasping.
In the body, speech, and mind, various experiences of
discomfort and illness
Arise one after the other without any kind of ground.
Hope for and clinging to the good will arise;
Fear of the bad, seeing dangers as real, will arise.
All of these [experiences] cause one to become trapped on a narrow
precipice of pitfalls and errors.

The all-encompassing, general outline, the essential point of the path:
The three—happiness, suffering, and neutral—all the experiences,
Definitively recognize them all as not truly existent,
like false impressions of experiences.
Then relax without rejecting and accepting.
This [set of instructions] is the sole wisdom that cuts through all
pitfalls.

If one is far away from a noble guide,
Then hold these five categories as the supreme path.
If one exerts too much effort in the practice single-pointedly,
Then the power of the mind will decrease, and only focused
mindfulness becomes established.
While the body is human, the mind becomes like an animal's mind;
Some will be lost in mental instability.
Therefore, rely on a noble guide without separation.

མདོར་ན་འདི་དག་སེམས་ལ་ལམ་བྱེད་སྐབས༔
ཐར་བ་རྣམ་མཁྱེན་ལམ་ལ་སྦྱ་ཙམ་ཡང༔
ཉེ་བ་མ་ཡིན་ཕྱིར་ན་ཡུན་རིང་པོར༔
བརྩོན་འགྲུས་དྲག་པོས་ཉམས་སུ་བླང་ན་ཡང༔
མི་ཚེ་སྟོང་ཟད་ཆུད་དུ་ཟ་བར་ངེས༔
ཤེས་པར་གྱིས་ཤིག་སྐལ་བཟང་སྐྱེས་བུ་རྣམས༔
ཤེས་རིག་རྡོ་རྗེ་རྣོན་པོའི་རྒྱུད་ལས༔ མ་དག་པ་སེམས་ལ་ལམ་བྱེད་པའི་སྐབས་ཏེ་དང་པོའོ༔

II.

ཤེས་རབ་རྡོ་རྗེ་རྣོན་པོ་མངོན་གྱུར་ནས༔
རིག་པ་ལུང་མ་བསྟན་གྱི་གཞི་ལས་འཕགས༔
ཅི་ཡང་མ་ཡིན་སྨྲ་བསམ་བརྗོད་ལས་འདས༔
བསྒོམ་བཅོས་དགག་སྒྲུབ་མེད་པར་རང་ཡན་པ༔
ཤེས་རིག་རྡོ་རྗེ་རྣོན་པོར་ལྷུན་གྱིས་གྲུབ༔

ལྟ་སྒོམ་སྤྱོད་པ་གཞི་ལམ་འབྲས་བུའི་ཆོས༔
སྐྱབས་སེམས་ཕར་ཕྱིན་དྲུག་དང་ལྷ་སྔགས་དལ༔
མ་ལུས་རྡོ་རྗེ་རྣོན་པོར་གཅིག་དྲིལ་རྫོགས༔

མ་རིག་ཉོན་མོངས་བདུད་ཀྱི་དབང་གྱུར་པའི༔
སེམས་ཅན་གང་དག་སྐད་ཅིག་བྱེ་བྲག་ཕྱེད༔
རྣམ་མཁྱེན་རྫོགས་པའི་སངས་རྒྱས་མངོན་དུ་བྱེད༔
ལྷར་བཅས་སྐྱེ་དགུའི་བསོད་ནམས་ཞིང་སར་འགྱུར༔

ཤེས་རིག་རྡོ་རྗེ་རྣོན་པོའི་རྒྱུད་ལས༔ ལྷག་མཐོང་རྡོ་རྗེ་རྣོན་པོའི་རང་ཞལ་མངོན་དུ་བྱེད་པའི་སྐབས་ཏེ་གཉིས་པའོ༔

In brief, while taking mind as the path,
One is not even as close as a hair to the path of
liberation and omniscience.
Even if, for a long period of time,
One is practicing [in this way] with intense diligence,
Life would be squandered and wasted.
Understand this, fortunate ones.

From the *Sharp Vajra of Awareness Tantra*, the first chapter on taking the impure mind as a path.

II. Direct Seeing: Actualizing the True Face of the Sharp Vajra

When the sharp vajra of wisdom is actualized,
Awareness is exalted from the undifferentiated ground.
It is nothing whatsoever, beyond words, thoughts, and description.
Without contrived meditation, nor accepting and rejecting,
naturally free,
It is spontaneously present as the sharp vajra of wisdom.

View, meditation, conduct, ground, path, fruition,
Taking refuge, developing bodhicitta, six paramitas, deity,
mantra, mandala—
They are all completely distilled into one essence within the sharp vajra.

Then, [even though] controlled by the maras of unawareness
and kleshas,
Sentient beings are realized in a single instant,
Omniscient perfect buddhahood is actualized,
And [they] become the field of merit for all beings, including gods.

From the *Sharp Vajra of Awareness Tantra*, the second chapter on direct seeing, actualizing the true face of the sharp vajra.

III.

སོར་རྟོག་ཤེས་རིག་རྡོ་རྗེ་རྣོན་པོ་ཡིས༔
བདག་རྟོག་འཁོར་བའི་རི་བོ་བཅོམ་པར་བྱེད༔
འཁོར་བའི་རྩ་བ་ང་རུ་འཛིན་པ་ཡི༔
བྱུང་གནས་འགྲོ་གསུམ་མིང་དང་དངོས་པོར་གཞིག༔
ཡུལ་མེད་སྟོང་པ་ཉིད་དུ་ཐག་ཆོད་པ༔
གང་ཟག་བདག་མེད་གཏན་ལ་ཕེབས་པའོ༔

བདག་དང་ཡུལ་གྱི་མིང་གི་གདགས་གཞི་བཙལ༔
ཡུལ་མེད་སྟོང་པ་ཉིད་དུ་ཐག་ཆོད་དེ༔
དངོས་པོ་ཐམས་ཅད་རྫུལ་ཕྲན་ཆ་མེད་ནས༔
རང་བཞིན་མེད་པར་སྟོང་པའི་དང་ཚུལ་བརྟག༔

འདི་སྣང་ཕྱི་སྣང་སྐྱེ་ལམ་སྣང་སྲིད་ཆོས༔
ཡུལ་མེད་སྟོང་པའི་དབྱིངས་སུ་ཐག་ཆོད་བྱས༔
ལས་འབྲས་དགེ་སྡིག་ལྷ་འདྲེའི་ཕན་གནོད་པ༔
ཡུལ་མེད་ཟང་ཐལ་དང་དུ་ཐག་ཀྱང་གཅོད༔

སངས་རྒྱས་དང་ནི་སངས་རྒྱས་ཞིང་བཀོད་པ༔
ཁམས་གསུམ་འཁོར་བའི་སྣང་སེམས་ཡུལ་དང་བཅས༔
བྱུང་གནས་འགྲོ་གསུམ་གཞི་དང་རྩ་བ་བཅད༔
ཐམས་ཅད་ཡུལ་མེད་སྟོང་པ་ཉིད་ཀྱི་དང༔
ཁ་ཙམ་མིན་པར་དོན་གྱིས་ཤེས་པར་གྱིས༔

III. Actualization of the Ground Dharmakaya

The sharp vajra of discriminating awareness
Destroys the samsaric mountain of self-concept.
The root of samsara, self-grasping—
Analyze its origin, residence, destination as well as name and actuality,
Determining that it is objectless and empty.
This is the establishment of the selflessness of the individual.

Seek the basis for labeling of self and object.
Determining that it is objectless and empty, then
Analyze how all things, all the way down to partless particles,
Are lacking intrinsic nature and are empty.

Appearances of this life and the next life, as well as dreams,
Are determined to be objectless within empty space.
Karmic cause and effect, virtue and vice, benefit from gods,
 and harm from demons
Are all determined to be objectless and transparent.

Buddhas and the buddha fields,
The objects of appearances and experiences of the three samsaric realms,
Determine that the ground and root of the three—origin, residence,
 destination—are non-existent.
All of them are objectless and empty.
Realize this meaning, not just by saying [the words].

སྟོང་ཆེན་ནམ་མཁའ་འཁོར་བའི་སྣང་གཞིར་གྲུབ༔
ཐམས་ཅད་ཡུལ་མེད་ནམ་མཁའི་འཁོར་ཡུག་ཏུ༔
ཐག་བཅད་ནམ་མཁའ་ཀུན་གྱི་གཞི་རུ་གྲུབ༔
ནམ་མཁའ་རྣམ་པར་དག་པ་སངས་རྒྱས་ཏེ༔
གཞི་ཡི་ཆོས་སྐུ་བདེ་གཤེགས་སྙིང་པོ་ལགས༔
དེས་ན་ཐམས་ཅད་སྟོང་པ་ཉིད་དུ་རྟོགས༔
བདག་མེད་ཤེས་རིག་རྡོ་རྗེ་སྙིང་པོ་ཉིད༔
མངོན་གྱུར་གཞིར་གནས་རིག་པ་ཚད་དུ་ཕེབས༔

དེ་མཐར་རེ་དོགས་འཛིན་ཞེན་ཕྱུག་རྫིབ་ཕྱིར༔
སྒོ་གསུམ་རྡོ་རྗེ་གསུམ་དུ་གསལ་བཏབ་ནས༔
ཆིངས་ཆེན་གསུམ་གྱི་མན་ངག་གནད་ལྡན་པས༔
གཉན་ཁྲོད་དག་ཏུ་ངེས་མེད་རྒྱུ་བྱས་ནས༔
གཅེས་འཛིན་ལུས་ཀྱི་མཆོད་སྦྱིན་མཆོག་ཏུ་བྱ༔
དེ་ཡིས་རེ་དང་དོགས་པའི་རྫུན་ཕྱུག་རྫིབ༔

ཤེས་རིག་རྡོ་རྗེ་སྙིང་པོའི་རྒྱུད་ལས༔ གཞིའི་ཆོས་སྐུ་མངོན་དུ་བྱེད་པའི་སྐབས་ཏེ་གསུམ་པའོ༔

IV.
སྣང་སྲིད་ཀུན་གྱི་ངོ་བོ་སྟོང་པ་ཉིད༔
སྟོང་ཆེན་ལམ་གྱི་ངོ་བོར་ལྷུན་གྱིས་གྲུབ༔

ངོ་བོ་ཆོས་སྐུ་བདེ་གཤེགས་སྙིང་པོ་ནི༔
འཁོར་འདས་གཉིས་ཀྱིས་བཅོས་དང་བསྒྱུར་དུ་མེད༔
སྤྲོས་པའི་མཐའ་བྲལ་རྣམ་ཐར་སྒོ་གསུམ་ལྡན༔
སྐུ་ལྷ་རིགས་ལྷ་ཡེ་ཤེས་རྣམ་ལྷ་དང༔
ཞིང་ལྷ་ཡབ་ལྷ་ཡུམ་ལྷ་དཀོན་མཆོག་གསུམ༔

The great emptiness, space, is the ground of samsaric appearances.
All things are as objectless as the sphere of space;
Determine that space is the ground of all.
The pure space is buddhahood.
It is the ground dharmakaya, buddha nature;
Therefore, realize all phenomena are emptiness.
The sharp vajra of awareness, no-self—
Actualizing that is the full maturity of ground-residing awareness.

Afterwards, in order to collapse the structure of grasping and
clinging to hope and fear,
Visualize one's three gates as three vajras.
With the essential points, pith instructions, of the three great bindings,
Travel aimlessly through the haunted ground and
Engage in the supreme generosity of offering this cherished body.
This will collapse the false structure of hope and fear.

From the *Sharp Vajra of Awareness Tantra*, the third chapter on the actualization of the ground dharmakaya.

IV.
Establishing the Characteristic and Quality of the Ground

The nature of all apparent existence is emptiness.
The great emptiness is naturally complete within the nature of the path.

The essence, dharmakaya-buddha nature,
Is beyond being altered or contrived by either samsara or nirvana,
Free from all conceptual extremes, endowed with the
three gates of liberation.
The five kayas, five families, five wisdoms,
Five buddha fields, five fathers, five mothers, three jewels,

རྩ་གསུམ་རིགས་དང་དཀྱིལ་འཁོར་དབང་བསྙེན་པ༔
མ་ཧཱ་ཡོ་གའི་ངོ་བོ་ལྷུན་གྱིས་གྲུབ༔

ལུས་ཀྱི་ནང་གནས་བཀོད་པ་ལྷ་ལྷན་དང༔
རྩ་རླུང་ཐིག་ལེ་སྦྱང་བསྒྱུར་འབར་འཛག་ལམ༔
དབང་དང་དགའ་བཞིར་བཅས་པ་ཐམས་ཅད་ཀུན༔
བདེ་གཤེགས་སྙིང་པོའི་ལྷུན་གྲུབ་ཆ་ལས་འཕྲུལ༔

མདོར་ན་ཆོས་སྐུ་མཚན་མ་བྲལ་བའི་དབྱིངས༔
འཁོར་བའི་སྒྲོ་བསྐུན་མེད་ཚུལ་མཚན་མས་བཅིངས༔
གདུལ་བྱ་རྟག་འཛིན་ཅན་རྣམས་ཁ་དྲངས་ཕྱིར༔
མངོན་པར་ཞེན་པ་དྲུག་ལས་བཟློག་པའི་ཕྱིར༔
གསལ་དག་སྟོང་པ་གསུམ་གྱིས་རུ་བཟློག་བྱེད༔

དེ་ཕྱིར་ཀུན་རྫོབ་བཅོས་མའི་ཆོས་དེ་དག༔
དཔེར་ན་རྒྱ་མཚོར་ཆུ་ཕྲན་སྦྲོ་བསྲུ་བཞིན༔
བདེ་གཤེགས་སྙིང་པོས་ཐེག་ཀུན་སྦྲོ་བསྲུ་བྱེད༔
དེ་ཕྱིར་གཞི་ཡི་རྫོགས་པ་ཆེན་པོར་གྲགས༔

རྟག་ཆད་མཐར་ཞེན་མུ་སྟེགས་ལམ་ཆོལ་བ༔
སྣང་སེམས་མངོན་ཞེན་འཐས་པས་རྒྱུད་འཁྲུལ་འཁོར༔
གང་ཟག་བདག་མེད་ལམ་བྱེད་ཉན་ཐོས་པ༔
རྟེན་འབྲེལ་ལུགས་ལྡོག་སྟོང་འཛིན་རང་རྒྱལ་ལམ༔
སྣང་སྲིད་སེམས་སུ་བལྟ་བའི་སེམས་ཙམ་པ༔
ཐམས་ཅད་སྟོང་པར་འཛིན་པའི་དབུ་མ་པ༔

The three roots, enlightened families, mandalas,
empowerment, propitiation—
They are all naturally complete within the nature of Maha Yoga.

In the body, with the five arrangements,
The purification and transmutation of the nadi, prana, and bindu;
the path of blazing and dripping;
Empowerments; and the four [kinds of] bliss
Are all spontaneously present as the play of buddha nature.

In essence, dharmakaya is the space, free from all the signs,
Yet, in accordance with samsara, the bondage of names and forms
[is taught]
In order to lead those who, grasping at permanence, are to be tamed.
In order to refrain from the six fixations,
The entrance of samsara will be blocked by the three:
clarity, purity, and emptiness.

Therefore, all the contrived, provisional reality,
Just like all the rivers come and return to the ocean,
Along with the yanas, manifest and dissolve into buddha nature.
Therefore, this is called the ground Great Completion.

Seeking the path of tirthikas is attachment to eternalism and nihilism.
Due to utterly clinging to appearances and experiences, the mindstream
is deluded in samsara.
The shravakas take selflessness of the individual as the path;
The path of pratyekabuddhas reverses interdependent origination and
holds onto emptiness;
The Cittamatrins view all apparent existence as mind;
The Madhyamakins apprehend everything as emptiness;

གཙང་སྦྲ་གཙོར་སྟོན་ཡུལ་ཞེན་ཀྲི་ཡ་པ༔
ལྟ་སྤྱོད་གོང་འོག་འདྲེས་པའི་ཨུ་པ་ཡ༔
ཡུལ་གོལ་རང་རྒྱུད་བལྟ་བའི་མ་ཧཱ་དང༔
དབྱིངས་ཡེ་རྒྱུ་འབྲས་མངོན་སྙོམས་ཨ་ནུའི་ལམ༔
དམ་ཡེ་ཐ་དད་རང་རྒྱུད་ཡོ་ག་པ༔
དེ་དག་རྣམས་ཀྱི་ས་ལམ་ཉམས་རྟོགས་ཀུན༔
རྫོགས་པ་ཆེན་པོའི་ལྷུན་གྲུབ་ཉག་ཕྲན་རེ༔
རྒྱ་མཚོའི་ཆུར་བླངས་རྒྱ་མཚོར་འཛིན་པ་བཞིན༔
འདི་དོན་རྟོགས་པས་ཐེག་ཀུན་ཉམ་རེ་ཐག༔

ཤེས་རབ་ཡེ་ཤེས་མངོན་གྱུར་རིག་པའི་དབྱིངས༔
སྤང་ཐོབ་བྲལ་བའི་སངས་རྒྱས་ཀུན་ཏུ་བཟང༔
འཁོར་འདས་ལམ་གྱི་ངོ་བོ་རྫོགས་པ་ཆེ༔
ཡིན་ཕྱིར་ལམ་གྱི་རྫོགས་པ་ཆེན་པོར་གྲགས༔

རྒྱུ་ཡི་ཐེག་ཀུན་འབྲས་བུར་སྙོམ་པའི་ས༔
བདེ་གཤེགས་སྙིང་པོ་མངོན་གྱུར་ཀུན་བཟང་ཉིད༔
འཁོར་བའི་སྣང་སེམས་སྐུ་དང་ཡེ་ཤེས་སུ༔
མ་སྤང་རང་གྲོལ་རྒྱལ་ཀུན་བཀའ་ཚད་མ༔
དེ་ལས་འབྲས་བུར་སྙོམས་སེམས་ཨ་ཐང་ཆད༔
དེ་ཕྱིར་ཆོས་རྣམས་ཀུན་གྱི་འབྲས་བུར་གྱུར༔
འབྲས་བུའི་རྫོགས་པ་ཆེན་པོར་ལྷུན་གྱིས་གྲུབ༔

The Kriya Yogis emphasize cleanliness and are attached to objects;
The Upaya tantrikas mix the view of the upper and lower tantras;
The Yoga tantrikas regard samayasattva and jnanasattva as
intrinsically separate.
Maha Yoga mistakenly perceives objects as real;
The path of Anu Yoga conceives space and wisdom as cause and effect;
All their experiences and realizations of ground and paths
Are merely one speck of the spontaneous presence of
the Great Completion,
Like scooping water from the ocean, and thinking it is the ocean.
Realizing this, all other vehicles seem pitiful.

Wisdom and primordial wisdom are actualized as the
expanse of awareness.
Beyond accepting and rejecting, the Buddha Samantabhadra,
The essence of samsara, nirvana, and path, is
the Great Completion.
Therefore, this is renowned as the path Great Completion.

All the causal vehicles boast of the fruition without achieving it.
Here, the actualization of buddha nature is Samantabhadra itself.
All the samsaric appearances and mind are self-liberated as kayas and
wisdom
Without abandoning them. This is the authentic word of the buddhas.
Other than that, all the supposed fruitions of the other yanas
are exhausting.
Therefore, this is the fruition of all Dharmas.
It is spontaneously present as the fruition Great Completion.

སྲིད་དང་ཞི་བའི་མཐའ་རུ་མ་ལྷུང་བར༔
མཁྱེན་དང་གཟིགས་པའི་ཡེ་ཤེས་རྒྱལ་ཆེན་འབར༔
མིང་གི་འཇུག་སྒོ་ཐ་དད་མ་གྲུབ་ཀྱང༔
གདུལ་བྱའི་དོན་དུ་མིང་གི་ཐ་སྙད་གདགས༔

ཤེས་རིག་རྡོ་རྗེ་སྔོན་པོའི་རྒྱུད་ལས༔ གཞི་རང་གི་མཚན་ཉིད་དང་ཡོན་ཏན་གཏན་ལ་དབབ་པའི་སྐབས་ཏེ་བཞི་བའོ༔

V.

དེ་ཕྱིར་ཀ་དག་ཆེན་པོའི་རོལ་པ་ལས༔
མ་དག་འཁོར་བའི་སྣང་སེམས་མཆེད་པ་ནི༔

བདག་རྟོག་ཕྲ་བས་ཤེས་རབ་ཡེ་ཤེས་སྒྲིབ༔
གཞི་ཡི་མདངས་གདངས་ལྷུམས་སུ་ནུབ་པ་ལས༔
ཕྱི་གདངས་འཁོར་བའི་ཀུན་གཞི་ལུང་མ་བསྟན༔
བེམ་སྟོང་མཁའ་ལས་གསལ་བའི་ཆ་མཚོན་ཞིང༔
ངར་འཛིན་ཤེས་པ་སྣང་སེམས་མཆེད་གཞིར་ལངས༔
ཡིད་ཉིད་གཅིག་པུ་འཆར་རུང་གཞིར་གྲུབ་ནས༔
རྣམ་པར་ཤེས་པ་དྲུག་གི་གཡོ་འགྲུ་ལས༔
མ་ངེས་སྣང་ཡུལ་སྒྱུ་མའི་འཕྲུལ་བཞིན་སྣང༔

སོ་ཟིན་མེད་པར་སྤུ་རྩེ་རླུང་བསྐྱོད་བཞིན༔
འཕྲུལ་གཡོ་འབྱེད་སྤུད་སྒྱུར་བྱེད་རླུང་ལྷ་ཡིས༔
མ་དག་བསྐལ་བ་ཆགས་གནས་འཇིག་སྟོང་བྱེད༔
སྒོ་ལྔའི་རྣམ་ཤེས་གཟུང་བ་ཡུལ་དུ་མཆེད༔
ཡིད་ཤེས་ཕྲ་བའི་འགྲུ་རྟོག་འཛིན་པར་ལངས༔

Without falling into the extremes of existence and peace,
The great potential energy of knowledge and primordial wisdom blazes.
Even though all these vehicles and their entrances don't exist separately,
They are named for the benefit of those to be tamed.

From the *Sharp Vajra of Awareness Tantra*, the fourth chapter on establishing the characteristic and quality of the ground.

V. Self-Liberation of Duality

Therefore, from the display of the great original purity,
The appearances and experiences of impure samsara arise.

The subtle self-concept veils wisdom and insight.
While the natural expression of the ground settles in the womb,
The outer expression is the undifferentiated base of samsara.
From that dead empty space, the aspect of clarity manifests.
The self-grasping consciousness arises as a base for experiences and
appearances to unfold.
Only the mind itself exists as a potential basis for
everything to arise.
From that, the six consciousnesses move.
Indefinite apparent objects appear as an illusory show.

Without any stability, just like the tip of a hair is moved by the wind,
The five winds of manifestation, movement, separation,
gathering, and transmutation
Cause creation, maintenance, destruction, and voidness of the eons.
The five sense-consciousnesses engage with perceived objects.
The movement of subtle consciousness arises as the perceiver, the
subject.

ཉིན་གཅིག་ཟླ་བའི་བསྐལ་པ་གྲངས་མེད་ཐུབ༔
ཡིད་ཀྱི་ཁམས་སུ་ཡོ་ལོག་ཉིན་སྣང་དང༔
ཀུན་གཞིའི་ཁམས་སུ་ཡོ་ལོག་མཚན་སྣང་ཤར༔
གཉིད་དུ་ཐོགས་ཚེ་བསྐལ་བ་དབྱིངས་སུ་ཞིག༔

ཀུན་གཞི་གཟུགས་མེད་ཉོན་ཡིད་གཟུགས་ཀྱི་ཁམས༔
ཡིད་ཉིད་འདོད་པའི་ཁམས་སུ་ལྷུན་གྱིས་གྲུབ༔
ཁམས་གསུམ་ཕྱི་རུ་རྡུལ་ཙམ་སྲིད་མ་ཡིན༔

བདག་ལྟའི་རུ་ཏྲ་འཁོར་བའི་མ་ཏྲི་ཀ༔
ཁྲོད་ལུས་འདོད་ཁམས་ངག་ཀྱང་གཟུགས་ཀྱི་ཁམས༔
ཡིད་ནི་གཟུགས་མེད་སྐྱེ་མཆེད་སུ་བཞིར་གནས༔
ཤ་ཁྲག་རྡོད་དབུགས་དཀར་དམར་ཐིག་ལེ་དབྱིངས༔
འབྱུང་བཞི་ཉི་ཟླ་སྒྲ་གཅན་དང་བཅས་གྲུབ༔

བདག་མེད་ཤེས་རིག་རྡོ་རྗེ་སྟོན་པ་ཡི༔
ཤུགས་དང་རླབས་ཀྱིས་བསྒྲལ་ནས་དག་དབྱིངས་སུ༔
དྭངས་མ་སྐུ་དང་ཡེ་ཤེས་ཆེན་པོར་མངོན༔
འཁོར་བ་མ་སྤྱངས་སངས་རྒྱས་ཉིད་དུ་གྲོལ༔
བདག་ལྟ་མ་སྤྱངས་ལྷུན་གྲུབ་རོལ་བར་ཞི༔
ཤེས་རིག་རྡོ་རྗེ་སྟོན་པའི་རྒྱུད་ལས༔

གསང་བའི་གཟུང་འཛིན་གཏན་ལ་དབབ་ཅིང་རང་གྲོལ་གྱི་ཚུལ་བསྟན་པའི་སྐབས་ཏེ་ལྔ་པའོ༔

VI.

གཞི་དབྱིངས་དོན་གྱི་སངས་རྒྱས་དཔང་བཙུགས་ཏེ༔
སྨོན་ལམ་རྣམ་པར་དག་པའི་སྟོབས་བསྐྱེད་ནས༔
རྣམ་མཁྱེན་སངས་རྒྱས་ས་རུ་དམ་བཅའ་བཞག༔

Countless subtle eons dissolve even within one day.
Entering into the sphere of the mind is the waking state.
Entering into the sphere of alaya is the sleeping state.
When moving toward sleep, an eon of time dissolves into space.

Alaya exists as the formless realm, klesha consciousness exists
as the form realm,
Mind itself spontaneously exists as the realm of desire.
The three worlds do not exist outside; not even one speck of dust.

The Rudra of self-concepts is the Matramkah of samsara.
Your body exists as the realm of desire, your speech is the realm of form,
Your mind exists as the four formless absorptions.
Your flesh, blood, heat, white and red bindus,
Exist as the four elements, sun, moon, Rahula, and so forth.

The sharp vajra of no-self
Liberates [Rudra] by its power and splendor, and in the pure expanse,
The subtle enlightened body and great primordial wisdom are
actualized.
Without abandoning samsara, the liberation of buddhahood [occurs].
Without abandoning self-view, everything dissolves into the display of
spontaneous presence.

From the *Sharp Vajra of Awareness Tantra*, the fifth chapter on establishing the secret duality of subject and object, and the way that self-liberation occurs.

VI.
Revealing Clear Distinctions and Vital Points of the Practice

Now calling upon the actual Buddha of the primordial ground
as a witness,
Generating the power of pure aspiration,
Commit to the buddhahood of omniscience.

དུས་ཀུན་འཆི་སྨྲ་ངས་དང་ནི་སྨྲ་བསྒྱུ་ཡིཿ
མན་ངག་གནད་ལ་བསླབ་པ་མཆོག་ཏུ་གཅེསཿ

ཀུན་གཞིའི་དབྱིངས་སྒྱུར་ཆོས་སྐུ་ཀུན་ཏུ་བཟངཿ
ཡིད་ཤེས་དབྱིངས་སྒྱུར་ཤེས་རབ་ཆེན་པོ་ཉིདཿ
སེམས་ཉིད་མངོན་སྒྱུར་རིག་པ་ལམ་གྱི་མཆོགཿ
རྣམ་ཤེས་མངོན་སྒྱུར་ཡེ་ཤེས་རྩལ་ཏུ་འབརཿ
སེམས་ཅན་ངོ་བོ་མངོན་སྒྱུར་སངས་རྒྱས་ཉིདཿ
མ་དག་སྣང་སེམས་ཟད་པ་གྲོལ་བ་དངོསཿ
གོ་བ་གཤིས་ཐོག་ཐེབས་པ་རྟོགས་པར་ངེསཿ
དེ་ལྟར་ཤན་འབྱེད་གནད་ལ་མ་རྨོངས་པརཿ
ཉམས་ལེན་གནད་དུ་བསྒྲུན་པ་མཆོག་ཏུ་གལཿ

ཤེས་རིག་རྡོ་རྗེ་རྟོན་པོའི་རྒྱུད་ལསཿ ཉམས་ལེན་གྱི་གནད་དང་ཤན་འབྱེད་ཀྱི་འཕྲོང་བསྟན་པའི་སྐབས་ཏེ་དྲུག་པའོཿ

VII.
དེ་ལྟར་གནས་ལུགས་མངོན་སྒྱུར་རྫོགས་པ་ཆེའིཿ
ཡིན་ལུགས་ཚུལ་བཞིན་རྟོགས་པའི་ཤེས་རབ་ཀྱིསཿ
ལྟ་སྒོམ་སྤྱོད་པ་གཅིག་དྲིལ་གནད་ལྡན་བྱཿ

ལམ་གྱི་ལམ་མཆོག་མྱུར་ལམ་སྙིང་པོའི་ཆོསཿ
སྤྲུན་དང་མངོན་ཤེས་རྫུ་འཕྲུལ་རླབས་པོ་ཆེཿ
བདག་ཉིད་འཕོ་བ་ཆེན་པོའི་གྲོང་འཇུག་པའིཿ
ཐོད་རྒལ་ལམ་ལ་བསྟེན་པས་མྱུར་དུ་གྲོལཿ

At all times, training in dying, and drawing in and uniting,
It is important to practice their essential points.

The actualization of the expanse of alaya is the
dharmakaya Samantabhadra.
The actualization of the expanse of mind-consciousness is the great
wisdom.
The actualization of nature of mind is the supreme
path of awareness.
From the actualization of consciousness, the potential energy of
primordial wisdom blazes.
The actualization of the nature of sentient beings is the Buddha.
Exhaustion of impure appearances and experiences is true liberation.
Arriving at the understanding of the natural state is realization.
Likewise, without being ignorant of the vital point
of clear distinctions,
It is important to strike the vital points of the practice.

From the *Sharp Vajra of Awareness Tantra*, the sixth chapter on revealing clear distinctions and vital points of the practice.

VII. How to Practice the Path of the Luminosity: Leaping-over

Likewise, actualization of the nature of reality is
the Great Completion.
By the wisdom that properly realizes such truth,
One should synthesize view, meditation, and conduct into
one essential point.

The supreme path of all paths, the shortcut, the essential Dharma,
Endowed with the splendid wisdom-eye, direct perception,
and siddhis;
The great transference of consciousness;
The path of leaping-over: one would be swiftly liberated by relying on it.

ཤེས་པ་དང་པོ་ཡུལ་དུ་མཆེད་པ་ཡིས༔
སྙིགས་མའི་སྣང་བ་བཙན་ཐབས་ཉིད་དུ་ནི༔
དྭངས་མའི་དབྱིངས་སུ་འཕོ་བའི་གདམས་པ་སྟེ༔

ཤེས་པ་དང་པོ་འོད་གསལ་སྣང་བ་རུ༔
མཆེད་དེ་ཤེས་རབ་མིག་ལ་ལྟད་མོར་མཐོང༔
སྣང་བ་འོད་གསལ་ཆེན་པོར་མཆེད་དེ་འཕེལ༔
རིག་པ་བཙུད་དུ་སྨིན་པའི་ཕྱག་རྒྱར་ངོམས༔
སྣང་སེམས་ཟད་པའི་ཆོས་ཉིད་དབྱིངས་སུ་བརྒྱལ༔

འཕོ་ཆེན་གཞོན་ནུ་བུམ་སྐུར་སངས་རྒྱས་ཏེ༔
རྟགས་ཀྱང་མཁའ་ལ་མཁའ་ཐིམ་ཇི་བཞིན་དང༔
ཚེ་དང་དུས་ལས་ཚད་ཐོགས་མཐར་མི་ཐུག༔

འཇའ་ལུས་དྭངས་མར་གྲོལ་བ་རྣམ་གསུམ་འབྱུང༔
ཉམས་སྣང་བཟང་ངན་མ་ངེས་སྣ་ཚོགས་ཀྱིས༔
བདེ་དང་སྡུག་བསྔལ་རིམ་པ་བཞིན་དུ་འབྱུང༔
ཐམས་ཅད་རེ་དོགས་མེད་པའི་དབྱིངས་སུ་བསྐྱལ༔

དེ་ལྟར་ལམ་མཐར་མ་ཕྱིན་སྐྱེས་བུ་དག༔
ལྟ་སྒོམ་གནད་རྟོགས་ཐེ་བྱ་ཚང་འཛུག་ལྟར༔
འཆི་སྲིད་ངོས་ཟིན་སྒེག་མོའི་བརྟན་བལྟ་དང༔
གནས་ལུགས་ངོས་ཟིན་སྤུར་འདྲེས་མིར་འཕྲད་དང༔
འོད་གསལ་དབྱིངས་ཞུགས་མ་པང་བུ་འཇུག་དང༔
གདམས་པའི་འཕྲོ་མཐུད་འདྲེན་ཆུར་ཞ་འཛུགས་དང༔
མངལ་གྱི་སྒོ་འགག་ཉེས་ཅན་བཙོན་ཐར་སོགས༔

The first moment of consciousness arising into objects
Creates contaminated appearances. Forcefully
Transforming them into pure dharmadhatu is the
pith instruction of transference.

The first consciousness arising as the appearance of clear light
Will become a spectacle for the wisdom-eye.
Appearances will arise and increase as the great luminosity.
Awareness will ripen as essence, and manifest and display as mudras.
The expansive nature of reality, where appearances and experiences are
exhausted, will be reached.

One will be awakened into the great transference,
the youthful vase body.
As a sign, it would be like space dissolves into space,
Beyond lifespan, time periods, and limitations.

Three types of liberation into the pure rainbow body will occur.
Because of various indefinite experiences,
Happiness and suffering will occur again and again.
One should take all of them into dharmadhatu without hope and fear.

Those who have not completed the path in such a way
Should understand the vital point of view and meditation like a swallow
entering its nest.
Recognize the bardo of dying as a beautiful woman looks at
her own reflection.
Recognize the nature of reality like meeting with a familiar person.
Enter into the expanse of luminosity like a child jumping into
its mother's lap.
Continue the pith instructions like installing a pipe to channel water.
Block the entrance to samsara, like a criminal released from prison.

དཔེ་དྲུག་གནད་དང་ལྡན་པ་མཆོག་ཏུ་ཤེས༔
དེ་ཡིས་གྲོལ་སྲིད་ཡང་ན་དབུགས་འབྱིན་འགྱུར༔

ཤེས་རིག་རྡོ་རྗེ་རྣོན་པོའི་རྒྱུད་ལས༔ འོད་གསལ་ཐོད་རྒལ་ཆེན་པོའི་ལམ་ཉམས་སུ་ལེན་པའི་ཚུལ་
བསྟན་པའི་སྐབས་ཏེ་བདུན་པའོ༔

VIII.

མཐར་ཐུག་རྣམ་པར་གྲོལ་བའི་འབྲས་བུ་ལ༔
གཞི་ཡི་ཆོས་སྐུ་བདེ་གཤེགས་སྙིང་པོ་ཉིད༔
ཆོས་སྐུ་གདོད་མའི་མགོན་པོར་ལྷུན་གྱིས་གྲུབ༔
ཐོབ་བྱ་གཞོན་ནུ་བུམ་པའི་སྐུ་ཉིད་དེ༔

དབང་པོ་རབ་ཀྱིས་ཚེ་གཅིག་མངོན་དུ་འགྱུར༔
འབྲིང་དང་ཐ་མས་སྐུ་དང་ཡོན་ཏན་དཔལ༔
རྣམ་དག་དབུགས་འབྱིན་ཞིང་ལྔའི་གཞི་རུ་བཞུགས༔

རྣམ་པ་ཀུན་ཏུ་གདུལ་བྱའི་དཔལ་མགོན་པོར༔
ཟླ་བ་ཆུ་ཟླ་ལྟ་བུར་ཅིར་ཡང་སྣང༔
གདངས་ཀྱི་འཁོར་བ་དབྱིངས་སུ་མ་ཞིག་པར༔
དབྱིངས་ཀྱི་ཡེ་ཤེས་རོལ་གར་རྒྱུན་མི་འཆད༔

ཤེས་རིག་རྡོ་རྗེ་རྣོན་པོའི་རྒྱུད་ལས༔ གཞི་ཡི་བཞུགས་ཚུལ་བསྟན་པའི་སྐབས་ཏེ་བརྒྱད་པའི་
བདག་ཉིད་ཅན་གྱིས་རྫོགས་སོ༔

It is essential to have the vital points of these six analogies.
By such means, it is possible that one will be liberated or relieved.

From the *Sharp Vajra of Awareness Tantra*, the seventh chapter on how to practice the path of the luminosity: leaping-over.

VIII. Revealing the Way Ground Abides

Ultimately, the result of complete liberation
Is the dharmakaya of the ground, buddha nature,
Spontaneously present as the dharmakaya Primordial Lord.
The object of attainment is the youthful vase body.

Those with the highest faculty will actualize it in one lifetime.
The middle and least ones will attain the glory of the kayas and qualities
And will be liberated in the ground of the five pure buddha realms.

Always appearing as lords for the benefit of those to be tamed,
[They are] like a moon reflecting its image in the water.
Until samsara, the radiance, dissolves into space,
The wisdom display of space will not cease.

From the *Sharp Vajra of Awareness Tantra*, the eighth chapter on revealing the way ground abides.

Colophon:

ཞེས་པ་འདི་ནི་ཁྲག་འཐུང་བདུད་འཇོམས་དཔའ་བོའི་ཡེ་ཤེས་སྒྱུ་མར་རོལ་པའི་སྣང་ཉམས་སུ་ཤར་བ་ལ༔ རེ་ཞིག་གི་དུས་སློབ་བུ་བྲ་བྲལ་པ་པད་མ་བཀྲ་ཤིས་དང་ཨོ་རྒྱན་རྡོ་རྗེ་རིག་པའི་སྨྱུ་གུ་བློ་གྲོས་དབང་པོ་རྣམས་ཀྱིས་ནན་ཏུ་བསྐུལ་བ་དོན་ཡོད་པའི་ཕྱིར་གཏན་ལ་ཕབ་པའི་དགེ་བས་ཁམས་གསུམ་གྱི་འཁོར་བ་དོང་ནས་སྤྲུགས་པར་གྱུར་ཅིག༔ དགེའོ༔ དགེའོ༔ དགེའོ༔ ལེགས་སོ༔ སརྦ་མངྒ་ལཾ།

Colophon:

This appeared as a vision of the wisdom illusory display of the heruka, Dudjom Pawo. At some point, to fulfill the zealous request of my students, the renunciate Padma Tashi, Orgyen Dorje, Rigpai Nyugu, and Lodro Wangpo, I wrote it down. May the virtue of this churn samsara from its depth. May it be virtuous. May it be virtuous. May it be virtuous. Well done! Sarva Mangalam!

About the Author

Anam Thubten grew up in Tibet and at an early age began to practice in the Nyingma tradition of Tibetan Buddhism. He is the founder and spiritual advisor of Dharmata Foundation and teaches widely in the United States and abroad. More information about Anam Thubten, including his teaching calendar, can be found online at dharmata.org. Anam Thubten's published books in English include:

Citadel of Awareness: A Commentary on Jigme Lingpa's Dzogchen Aspiration Prayer

Fragrance of Emptiness: A Commentary on the Heart Sutra

Into the Haunted Ground: A Guide to Cutting the Root of Suffering

A Sacred Compass: Navigating Life Through the Bardo Teachings

Choosing Compassion: How to be of Benefit in a World that Needs Our Love

No Self, No Problem

Several of these books have also been translated into various languages, including Korean, French, and German. In addition, Anam Thubten has authored several books and many articles in Tibetan.

www.ingramcontent.com/pod-product-compliance
Lightning Source LLC
Chambersburg PA
CBHW071855160426
43209CB00005B/1060
9781732020887